THE SPIRAL OF TIME SERIES

RAV DOVBER PINSON

THE MONTH of KISLEV

vol 9

REKINDLING HOPE
DREAMS & TRUST

IYYUN PUBLISHING

Published by IYYUN Publishing
232 Bergen Street
Brooklyn, NY 11217

http:/www.iyyun.com

Iyyun Publishing books may be purchased for educational, business or sales promotional use.
For information please contact: contact@IYYUN.com

Editor: Reb Matisyahu Brown

Developmental Editor: Reb Eden Pearlstein

Proofreading / Editing: Reb Levi Robin

Cover and book design: RP Design and Development

Cover image:
"Kislev" by Alex Greenfield from The Misaviv Hebrew Circle Calendar by Deuteronomy Press.
www.circlecalendar.com

pb ISBN 978-1-7338130-9-9

Pinson, DovBer 1971-
The Month of Kislev: Rekindling Hope, Dreams and Trust.
1.Judaism 2. Jewish Spirituality 3. General Spirituality

vol 9

THE MONTH of ב KISLEV

REKINDLING HOPE DREAMS & TRUST

INCLUDING ESSAYS ON THE HOLY DAYS OF CHANUKAH

IYYUN PUBLISHING

ב"ה

THE MONTH OF KISLEV

DEDICATION

THIS BOOK IS DEDICATED
IN LOVING MEMORY OF

MIRIAM ע"ה

BAT

GERSHON AND LEAH

BY HER DAUGHTER

HILLARY BARR

שתחי'

May the *neshamah* of this true
Eishet Chayil who brightened the world
when she was in it, continue to illuminate our
world from above.

May the *zechus*/merit of those learning
these words of Torah be a source
of blessing to all her descendants,
for life, health, prosperity and joy.

CONTENTS

CONTENTS

PART TWO: Essays on the Holy Days of Chanukah

OPENING

EACH MONTH OF THE YEAR RADIATES DISTINCT QUALITIES and provides unique opportunities for personal growth and spiritual illumination. Accordingly, every month has a slightly different climate and represents a particular stage in the 'story of the year' as expressed through the annual cycles of nature. The winter months call for practices and pursuits that are intrinsically different than those of the summer months. Some months are filled with Holy Days, some have only one, and others none. Each month therefore has its own natural and spiritual 'signature.'

According to the deeper levels of Torah, each month's distinct qualities, opportunities, and natural phenomena correspond to a twelve-part symbolic structure; the spiritual nature of each month is articulated in 12 points of light, which include: 1) a permutation of Hashem's Four-Letter name, 2) a verse from the Torah, 3) a letter of the Aleph Beis, 4) the meaning of the name of the month, 5) an experiential sense, 6) a Zodiac sign, 7) a tribe of Israel, 8) a body part, 9) a natural element, 10) a unit of successive Torah portions that are read during the month, 11) a season of the year, and 12) the Holy Days that occur during the month.

By reflecting on these twelve aspects, an ever-ascending spiral of insight, understanding, and practical action is revealed. Learning to navigate and harness the nature of change by holistically engaging with the cycles of time, adds a deeper sense of purpose and heightened presence to our lives.

The present volume will delve into the spiritual nature of the month of Kislev, according to these twelve categories.

NOTE: For a more comprehensive treatment of this 12-part system and the overarching dynamics of the "story of the year", an in-depth introduction has been provided in Volume One of this series, The Spiral of Time: Unraveling the Yearly Cycle.

THE MONTH OF KISLEV
Rekindling Trust, Hope & Dreams

KISLEV IS THE THIRD AND FINAL MONTH OF THE FALL SEASON in the Northern Hemisphere. Toward the end of this notoriously cold and wet month, something quite unique occurs and that is the waning of the moon closest to the winter solstice, making this the darkest point of the year, whether day or night. Although it will continue to get even colder over the next couple of months of the winter season, the sunlight does begin to shine slightly longer around this time, rising gradually higher in the sky, and lengthening the days. For six months from the beginning of the summer the days had become shorter and shorter, until usually by the end of Kislev this pattern reverses.

As the sun begins incrementally emerging from the darkness, it brings renewed hope, a rekindling of our dreams, and a trust in a better future. This is a manifestation of "Reflected Light", the spiritual light that is revealed during Kislev, the light that we can bring into the world. The physical return of daylight, and the psychological sense of increasing hope, are dual expressions of the metaphysical dynamic present in this month.

On a psychological level, Kislev is a time when our sense of being alone, which naturally arises during the previous month of Cheshvan, can start to feel less empowering, and more like being 'lonely'. At the end of Kislev there is a strong desire to get out and find some 'light', some connection with others, and to spend time with friends and family. This yearning for light and connection is an expression of the deeper longing for Divine Light and Divine connection. We are drawn to the Light that begins to manifest towards the end of the month — the Light of Chanukah.

Kislev gives us strength to have confidence and trust in the Divine Light, even when it is concealed; that eventually, Hashem's light will fully emerge and triumph, overcoming and eradicating the darkness. In our own lives, even when we are surrounded by darkness, whether physical, emotional, mental or spiritual — such as when we feel lost, disconnected, depressed, or alone — we can be empowered by keeping in mind that in the end, light will always rise up and prevail. This is certainly true so long as we actively seek it and do not give up in our quest for illumination. Indeed, often the light returns precisely *because of* the darkness that one is experiencing. The experience of existential dread, for example, can stimulate within us a deeper resolve to overcome fear and rekindle our aspirations and dreams. This is one way that darkness manifests for the sake of a greater light. In fact, such darkness can stimulate a higher light to be revealed. The deeper the abyss, the brighter the light we need to inwardly reveal in order to illuminate it. This is the idea of *Ohr Chozer* / reflected or returning light; it is the light that we can generate from within that initiates or contributes to a corresponding illumination from without. As will be explored in depth, this is represented by the act of lighting the Chanukah candles within the midst of the darkest point of the year.

As mentioned, Kislev is the final month of the fall. Weather-wise, it is much like the previous month of Cheshvan: dreary, rainy, chilly, and damp. Days and sunlight continue to recede and there can be a visceral sense of lethargy or even dread of winter cold. The majority of Kislev follows the same trajectory. The days continue to get shorter and colder until we reach the waning moon around the winter solstice, the darkest and longest night of the year, near the end of the month. At that point, a tiny glimmer of light returns and daylight gradually begins to replace the darkness of night. As such light begins to reemerge, a sense of hope returns. The spiritual work of Kislev involves connecting with that tiny glimmer of light, expanding it, and harnessing that glow of hope to dream of a brighter future.

Kislev gives us the *Koach* / power to tap into an inner reservoir of *Emunah* / faith and *Bitachon* / hope. This inner foundation allows us to extricate ourselves from the grip of darkness and the sense of impending doom so prevalent during the cold and dark season. It helps us take hold of the Light of HaKadosh Baruch Hu and kindle our lamps of hope, progress, creativity, movement, and growth. Together, we can fan the small glimmering lights hidden within the darkness until they are transformed into a bright and everlasting flame.

PERMUTATION OF HASHEM'S NAME

The Four Letter Essential Name, Yud-Hei-Vav-Hei (Hashem), is the Divine Source of all reality. The last three letters of the Name, Hei-Vav-Hei, create the word *Hoveh* / is. The root of this verb means, 'to bring into being'. The first letter of the Name, Yud, serves as a prefix to the last three letters: Yud-*HoVeH*. In this way, the Yud modifies the verb to represent a perpetual activity (see Iyov, 1:5). The Divine Name can thus be understood to mean, 'That Which is Continuously Bringing Being into Being'.

For numerous reasons, this Essential Name cannot be spoken. Therefore a common practice is to rearrange its four letters into an alternate construction that may be pronounced. This produces the word *Havayah*, which literally means 'Being-ness'. This aspect of the Name refers to the Ultimate Being, which is the Source and Substance of all that is. The Ultimate Being does not depend on anything else to exist. It gives rise to all past, present and future manifestations, thereby bringing all things into existence ex nihilo, i.e. *Yesh meAyin* / being from non-being. Accordingly, the individual words *Hayah* / was, *Hoveh* / is and *Yihyeh* / will be, are all encoded within the Essential Name.

As *HaVaYaH* is the Source of all Being and Time, it is thus connected with actual time. Because of this, each unique period in time is imbued with a special connection to the Essential Name. In terms of the months, this quality is expressed through a unique permutation of the four letters that comprise the Name. Each permutation communicates a different spiritual dynamic which is part of the Divine signature encoded within that particular month.

The sequence of letters in Hashem's Name which corresponds to the month of Kislev is Vav-Yud-Hei-Hei.* In the Name of Hashem there are two 'masculine' letters, otherwise called *Mashpi'im* / givers, and there are two 'feminine' letters, otherwise called *Mekablim* / receivers. The letters Yud (י) and Vav (ו), the smaller point and longer line-shaped letters, are the Mashpia letters. Yud is the higher Mashpia, and Vav the lower Mashpia.

* The vowels in the sequence of Hashem's name for the month of Kislev are Patach-Vav, Cholam-Yud, Kamatz-Hei, Patach-Hei.

The letter Hei (ה) is structured more like a receptacle, and the two Hei's in the Name similarly represent a higher Mekabel and a lower Mekabel. When the sequence of the Name of Hashem is in its 'correct' manifestation, Yud-Hei-Vav-Hei, then the movement is from the higher Mashpia (Yud) into the higher Mekabel (Hei), the 'father' and 'mother'. These 'parents' in turn give birth to the lower Mashpia (Vav) who unifies with the lower Mekabel (final Hei), thereby bringing reality from pure spiritual potential to actual manifestation in this world. In this way, we and the world receive Divine flow and vitality from Beyond the Name, the *Ohr Ein Sof* / Infinite Light. This Light must first become revealed in the higher Mashpia, where it is aroused and flows into the Higher Mekabel, cascading 'downward' until the *Shefa* / Divine influx reaches us. The movement of the Shefa and *Ohr* / light is in this case direct, from above to below. This is also called *Ohr Yashar* / direct light, a paradigm in which Light appears first, and then it travels and flows into the lower reaches, illuminating all possible corners of darkness.

In this month, the *Mashpia* / giving letters are both at the beginning, demonstrating that this sequence and this month is characterized by an emphasis on 'masculine' or active energy. What's more, their normal order is reversed. First comes the lower Mashpia, the Vav, and then the higher Mashpia, the Yud.

When the Shefa moves from a lower Mashpia to a higher letter, the pattern of *Ohr Chozer* / reflected light is in play. Again, this is the light that we generate from below. In this month's sequence, the light reflected from within the lower Mashpia (Vav) rises up to the higher Mashpia (Yud), where its inherent brightness and purity are exponentially intensified. Then, this radically magnified light is transmitted to the next letter, the Upper Hei and from there to the Lower Hei. As the sequence ends with a Lower Hei, the cycle of Shefa, which began with us below, can reconnect to its source Above, and can be fully received and assimilated into our consciousness and the world in a revealed way.

This is in contrast, for example, to the letter formation for the month of Cheshvan, which ends with the letter Yud, and is therefore lacking a final receiver. In that month the higher light of the Yud is not fully revealed. In Kislev, the Yud moves directly into the higher Mekabel, and then from there into the lower Mekabel. Therefore, in Kislev the higher Mashpia does reveal itself. However, as mentioned, the beginning of the sequence is generated by the letter Vav, which is a classic example of Ohr Chozer. Only later in the sequence, after the light from below has ascended, does the Light from Above move back downward into revelation. For this reason, the luminous miracles of Kislev are revealed only towards the end of the month, through the Yom Tov of Chanukah. Additionally, as these miracles are stimulated from below (Ohr Chozer), they do not appear 'on their own', as in the month of Nisan. In Kislev, it is we who, through our Emunah and steadfast Bitachon, act on our own initiative to bring the light back into circulation. This 'Ohr Chozer' stimulates and creates the vessels within which miracles can occur, as will be explored.

TORAH VERSE

THE UNIQUE SEQUENCE OF THE FOUR LETTER DIVINE NAME that shines during each month is encoded within a particular verse in the Torah (*Tikunei Zohar*, Hakdamah, 9b. *Eitz Chayim*, *Sha'ar* 44:7). In other words, there is a 'verse of the month' consisting of a four-word sequence, in which each word either begins or ends with the letters of the *Tziruf* / name-formation for that month (*Mishnas Chasidim*, Meseches Adar, 1:3). The meaning and context of the verse connected with each particular month is, of course, also part of the revelation of that month's guiding light.

The permutation of the Divine Name of Kislev, Vav-Yud-Hei-Hei, is found in the verse: וירא יושב הארץ הכנעני / *VaYar Yoshev haAretz haKenaani* / and the settlers of Canaan saw..." (*Bereishis*, 50:11).

This verse refers to the burial of Yaakov. According to tradition, Yaakov passed away during the days which were to eventually become the Yom Tov of Sukkos, and he was buried 70 days later, at the end of the month of Kislev, during the days that were to become Chanukah.

Our sages tell us that when Yaakov was being carried to his burial, 36 royal crowns of the descendants of Avraham were hanging from the coffin (שלשים וששה כתרים נתלו בארונו של יעקב: *Sotah*, 13a). Thirty-six is an important number relating to Kislev in general and to Chanukah in particular, as will be explored later on. For now suffice it to say that the 36 royal crowns represent the 36 lights that we kindle throughout the nights of Chanukah: on the first night, one light, on the second night, two lights, and so forth (1+2+3+4+5+6+7+8=36).

Although death and burial represent a state of concealment or absence of life and light, with regards to Yaakov we learn, "Yaakov our father, did not die" (*Ta'anis*, 5b). In other words, although his body was buried and there was an outward appearance of absence and grief, in reality, a deeper light was revealed. This light was revealed within the hearts of his descendants, as the above quote continues: "Just as his seed is alive, so is he" (*Ibid*). Yaakov lives on through his descendants, especially when they follow his path. When we actively manifest Yaakov's light, we earn the name *Klal Yisrael* / the Collective People of Israel, 'Yisrael' being Yaakov's higher spiritual name. Through the inner and outer achievements of the collective Klal Yisrael, Yaakov has become even more present in the world than when he was embodied as a single individual. The *Nitzutzim* / sparks of Yaakov's soul live on in the bodies of Klal Yisrael (*Tanya*, Igeres HaKodesh, 7. Also, נשיא הוא ראשי-תיבות ניצוצו של יעקב אבינו. Indeed, the *Nasi* / leader of Klal Yisrael embodies the sparks of Yaakov Avinu. See, *Keheles Yaakov*, Ma'areches Rebbe, regarding Rebbe Yehudah haNasi). Collectively, we continue to reveal his light today, as an *Ohr Chozer* / Reflected Light, an 'arousal from below'. From the place of his burial and his 'death' (the paradigm of 'below') the more powerful lights of Yaakov arise and are refracted out into the four corners of the universe.

LETTER

As the Torah, the 'Blueprint of Creation', is written in *Lashon haKodesh* / the Holy Tongue of Hebrew, the Sages teach that each of the 22 letters of the Aleph Beis contains a host of metaphysical creative potentials. According to the *Sefer Yetzirah*, a profound book of early Kabbalah that pays particular attention to the inner dimensions of the Hebrew letters, the 22 letters are divided into three categories: three "Mother Letters", seven "Double Letters" and 12 "Simple Letters". Each month is connected with one of the 12 Simple Letters.*

The simple letter associated with the month of Kislev is Samach (ס). *Samach* comes from the word *Somech* / supports, as in the verse

* For a more in-depth analysis of all three categories of Hebrew letters and their relationship to the calendar, please see the introductory volume in this series, *The Spiral of Time: Unraveling the Yearly Cycle*.

סומך ה לכל־הנפלים / *Somech Hashem l'Chol haNof'lim* / Hashem supports all the falling" (*Tehilim*, 145:14. *Berachos*, 4b. *Osyos d'Rebbe Akiva*, Samach). The shape of ס is a Chaf (כ), connected to a Vav (ו). Chaf has a numerical value of 20 and Vav is 6. When combined as a Samach, they are 26; the numerical value of the Name of Hashem. The message of Samach is thus, "Hashem is supporting us." When we have a deep trust that we are being supported, even if we fall into darkness, we can bounce back and return to the path of revealing even deeper light.

Addressing the letter Samach, the Zohar says, "Those who are falling lean on you" (*Zohar* 1, 3a). The supportive strength of Samach keeps the Nun, symbolizing the *Nofel* / falling dimension of Creation, from falling completely. Nun is the letter of the previous month of Cheshvan, and whereas Cheshvan gives us strength to get up after falling, Kislev and the letter Samech ensures that the Nun does not fall to begin with, or that if we are falling we can have faith that we are supported.

Samach itself is the numeral 60. According to *Halachah* / law, if a drop of non-Kosher milk accidently falls into a pot of kosher milk, and if that pot contains 60 or more times the volume of the un-kosher drop, the drop might be considered nullified and the entire pot of milk therefore remains kosher. In other words, under certain conditions a non-Kosher substance can become nullified within 60 parts of a Kosher substance (וכן אם הוא מין במינו כיון דליכא למיקם אטעמא משערים בס: *Shulchan Aruch*, Yorah De'ah, 98). When this nullification is in effect, not only is there is no longer any non-Kosher milk in the pot, but the non-Kosher milk that fell in has itself been transformed into Kosher milk, and one could recite a blessing over each ounce of milk there. In a similar way, under the spiritual influence of the letter Samach (60) in Kislev, darkness can be nullified and transformed into light, and 'falling' can be transformed into support and stability.

Samach, as the number 60, is also related to dreams: "Dreams are 1/60th of prophecy" (*Berachos*, 57b). Kislev is the month of dreams, as will be explored. It is also interesting to note that the letter Samach appears only once among the names of the sons of Yaakov, the *Shevatim* / tribes, and that is within the name of Yoseph, the "Master of Dreams".

Cheshvan's letter Nun, and Kislev's Samach, together spell the word *Nes* / miracle. It is specifically from within darkness and concealment, as present in these two months of encroaching darkness, that the miracle of Hashem's illumination can emerge most impactfully. In fact, concealment creates the conditions for revelation; darkness creates the contrast against which light shines. Additionally, when we have fallen like the shape of the letter Nun (see book on the month of Cheshvan), we can move toward the Samach, the *Somech* / Divine support, nullifying the negative effects of our fall and preventing any further descent. When we are secure, our hope grows and we can dream again and sense the miracles present in our life.* It is certainly a great miracle when darkness is transformed

* *Nes* in numeric value is 110, the same as the combination of the Names Mah and Ado-noi: *Eitz Chayim*, Sha'ar haKelalim, 11. *Mah*, literally translated as 'what', is a question mark, an uncertainty, potentially a place of darkness and exile. A Nes, on the other hand, is a movement out of a state of 'what'; for example if someone is puzzled by a surprising, miraculous event, they ask, *'What* just happened?' The answer is: 'It was *Ado-noi* — a revelation of Hashem's Presence.' Hence the move from question to answer, darkness to light.

into light — and this brings forth from within us "thanks-giving and praise", the mode of consciousness that characterizes the Yom Tov of Chanukah, the Holy Days of Kislev.

NAME OF THE MONTH

According to the Torah, names are very powerful (*Yumah*, 83b. *Tanchuma*, Hazinu. *Berachos*, 7b). Composed as they are of Hebrew letters, they represent and define the energy or attributes of that which is named (*Tanya*, Sha'ar haYichud ve-haEmunah, 1). Our names, for instance, unlock and reveal hidden potentials present within our own spiritual makeup. Similarly, names of other people, places, and periods of time provide subtle hints as to their deeper purpose or poetic significance. Additionally, changing one's name is akin to a kind of rebirth, and some might even say that a change of name initiates a change of *Mazal* (Rashi, *Bereishis*, 15:5. *Rosh Hashanah*, 16b. *Yerushalmi*, Shabbos, 6:39. Rama, *Yoreh Deah*, 335:10).

Each of the twelve months of the year has a distinct name, and every name has a meaning. According to our Sages, the current names we have for the months were imported to our tradition upon our return to Israel from the Babylonian Exile. (They can in fact be traced to ancient Babylonian or Akkadian names: see *Yerushalmi*, Rosh Hashanah, 1:2. *Medrash Rabbah*, Bereishis, 48:9. *Tosefos*, *Rosh Hashanah* 7a. *Even Ezra*, *Chezkuni*, Shemos. 12:2.) In the times before the Babylonian Exile the names of the months were mostly known by their number in the sequence of the year. For example, the month of Av was called the Fifth Month, and Cheshvan was known as the Eighth Month.*

Accordingly, before the Babylonian Exile Kislev had no distinct name, and was simply called 'the Ninth Month'. Only after the Exile was it called Kislev, as we can see in the post-Babylonian Exile books of *Nechemiyah* (1:1 .ויהי בחדש־כסלו) and *Zecharyah* (7:1). The secular root of this name is connected to the Akkadian name of the ninth month of the year, *Kislimu* / thickened or congealed, referring to the thickening of dust into clay, due to the abundance of rainfall in the previous month of Cheshvan. Chazal adopted this name, and now that Kislev is a Torah name for the month, we can tease out Torah meanings from its letters and etymology.

Chazal often derive teachings about words from other languages based on their Hebrew counterparts (Rav Yaakov Emdin, *Lechem Nikudim*, Avos, 2:14). This is done specifically with the names of months

* There are, however, a few months of the year that are named in the post Babylonian Exile writings in Tanach. Kislev is one of those months mentioned in the Book of *Nechemiyah* (ולסכ-שדחב יהיו. 1:1) and in the Book of *Zecharyah* (7:1). Nisan, too, is mentioned in Zecharyah (2:1), and the *Megilah* / Scroll of Esther (*Megilas Esther*, 8:9) mentions Sivan along with Adar (Ibid, 3:7), and Teves (Ibid, 2:16).

such as Nisan, which is originally not a Hebrew word; Chazal read *Nisin* from the word *Nes* / miracles (*Pesiktah Zutresah*, Bo, 12:2. *Medrash Lekach Tov,* Shemos 12:2. In the words of Rashi (*Berachos*, 56a), שע"י נסים נקרא ניסן / "Nisan is called *Nisan* because of the miracles"). More importantly, once a name becomes adapted as the Torah name for a month, it becomes enfolded within the context of Lashon haKodesh, and can then be subjected to the same methods of deeper interpretation.

כסלו / *Kislev* is related to a Hebrew word meaning trust: "Have I ever put כסלי / *Kisli* / my trust in gold?" (*Iyov,* 31:24. מבטחי. Ralbag, *ad loc.* האם שמתי בטחוני בזהב: *Metzudas David*). Another example is "...that they may כסלם / *Kislam* / trust in Hashem" (*Tehilim*, 78:7. כמו מבטחם *Even Ezra*). Kislev thus alludes to trust, confidence and hope; more commonly known as *Bitachon*. (More specifically, שהכסל הוא הבטחון מן הרע, והמבטח הוא אל הטוב / *Kesel* is trust that something will not be bad, while Bitachon is trust that something will be positive: *Malbim*, Iyov, ibid, Biur haMilos.)

Significantly, כסלו / *Kislev* is also related to the word כסה / *Kasa* to conceal or cover, and also related to the word meaning 'to protect'. All these meanings of *Kislev* are related to the shape of the letter of the month, Samach — a secure, protective, covering circle. When we truly put our trust in Hashem, we are surrounded and covered by Divine protection and goodness. In the words of King David, והבוטח בה' חסד יסובבנו / "He who trusts in Hashem, *Chesed* / kindness will surround him" (*Tehilim*, 32:10). Our trust is the *Kli* / vessel through which we draw down and ensure that we are always surrounded by Hashem's Chesed.

BITACHON — ACTIVE HOPE

General trust in life and in others is essential to our stable functioning and sustainable happiness. Even most mundane experiences in life call for some measure of trust. For example, you might arrange an important meeting with someone at a particular time and place. To do this you require trust, based on past experience, that the person will be there and at the appropriate time. Realistically, in such a situation, you may be 'taking a chance'. However, through trust, you feel completely confident that the meeting will come to fruition. This reflects an overall positive outlook on life.

Kislev reveals and inspires us towards a more powerful and empowering posture of *Bitachon* / trust in the Source of all Life. On the physical plane, which is a manifestation of the spiritual plane, Kislev contains both the longest and darkest night of the year, as well as the beginning of the return of the light and warmth of lengthening days. As the darkest season attains its crescendo with the winter solstice and waning moon of Kislev, a small but dramatic shift occurs and the light begins to expand. This mirrors our inner experience as well: at the peak of the darkness of our spiritual night, a small but powerful shift begins to occur and light begins to re-enter our psyche. This tiny glimmer of warm light is sufficient enough to relieve a person of his winter depression and stimulate a new sense of hope for a brighter future.

Emunah / belief is faith in HaKadosh Baruch Hu, the Creator of Life. On the deepest level, "We are all believers, the sons of believers." Belief is therefore innate — every effect deeply knows its Cause. But in addition to this 'natural' Emunah, we also need to have an active *Bitachon* / trust. What does it mean to have such Bitachon in HaKadosh Baruch Hu?

TWO LEVELS OF BITACHON

Bitachon can be understood on two levels. Having a mindset of Bitachon can mean, "I have *Bitachon* / trust that everything occurring in my life comes from Hashem." This level of Bitachon means I have deep trust that whatever is happening in my life, it is the will of Hashem. "Bitachon is a matter of trust that there is no coincidence in the world: everything that transpires under the sun results from His pronouncement, may He be blessed" (*Emunah u'Bitachon*, Chap. 2). In other words, *Bitachon is Emunah in action.* We have Emunah that Hashem is the primary and root cause of everything that happens in the world and in our life, and Bitachon is living that truth. In whatever we are going through, we recognize Hashem's Presence — this is Bitachon.

On a deeper level, there are aspects and areas of life for which we do not need trust, as we know some facts with certainty. But there are other aspects and areas of life in which trust is our only reliance and support. When you wake up early in order to meet someone at a particular time, you trust, based on past performance, that they will be on time. When in fact they do show up on time, you do not need 'trust' that they are there, as you already 'see' them.

Emunah is involved when you, your deepest self, 'sees' the truth of Hashem's presence and goodness. It is not merely an understanding of this truth, but it is as if you see it and are living with this truth (וצדיק באמונתו יחיה / a Tzadik *lives* with his Emunah: *Chabakuk*, 2:4. *Makos*, 24a). Bitachon is involved when you 'trust' that Hashem is present, even though you do not yet 'see' it. A person needs Bitachon especially when the meaning of his life trajectory or journey is not clear and apparent. He holds on with Bitachon that Hashem is there with him, and that whatever he is going through is for his ultimate best.

The forms of Bitachon mentioned above are somewhat passive. However, on an even deeper level, there is an aspect of Bitachon that can only be revealed if we choose to have it: this is 'active Bitachon'. On this level, we can become active participants in Hashem's revelation through our Bitachon. When we do so, Hashem responds in kind, returning the favor, so to speak. This level of Bitachon actually draws down the very goodness in which we are trusting.

With such active Bitachon we trust not only that everything in our lives comes from Hashem, but that since it comes from Hashem, it *will* in fact be good. HaKadosh Baruch Hu is the Creator of Life, and thus the very nature of the Creator (revealed in the act of creating) is to create, to give life and goodness; in the words of the Alter Rebbe, טבע הטוב להיטיב / the Nature of the Good (One) is to bestow goodness" (*Sha'ar haYichud ve'haEmunah*, 4. See also, *Shomer haEmunim* (haKadmon), 2:14. *Derech Hashem*, 2:1. *Da'as Tevunos*, beginning. *Shu't Chacham Tzvi*, 18). Bitachon is trust in the inherent *goodness* of Hashem, and furthermore that in the end this goodness will inevitably be revealed.

King David declares in Tehilim, והבוטח בה' חסד יסובבנו / "But he who trusts in Hashem shall be surrounded with goodness" (*Tehilim*, 32:10). The act of Bitachon itself draws down the *Chesed* / kindness, the giving, the goodness of HaKadosh Baruch Hu. Hashem is the Source of life and the opposite of life, the Creator of both light and darkness. Yet, a person who lives with Bitachon, in the goodness of

HaKadosh Baruch Hu, draws down more Divine goodness into their lives.

"Hashem is your shadow" (*Tehilim*, 121:5). Our shadow mimics our actions. Similarly, Hashem's relationship with us is like a shadow (*Keser Shem Tov*, Hos'fos, 60. *Shaloh*, Sha'ar haGadol, 22a). If we have active Bitachon in the goodness of Hashem and of His Creation, Hashem reciprocates and we elicit more and more goodness in our lives.

There is a Yiddish Chassidic expression coined by the Rebbe the Tzemach Tzedek: טראכט גוט וועט זיין גוט / "Think good and it will be good." Just thinking about the good, and that a given situation will be good, draws down the good. This is a perfect expression of the concept of Ohr Chozer, as we have been exploring in the context of Kislev.

Within a context of interpersonal relationships, enough cannot be said regarding the power of positive thinking. We generally find that people respond to our mindset in kind. For example, if we choose to be in a joyous disposition the people around us will tend to be more happy as well. And if we choose to walk around angry at others or with a negative attitude, people will respond in a like manner to us. The ways we think, speak, and act create an almost tangible 'vibe' around us. Whether consciously or not, people around us pick this frequency up and reciprocate accordingly, broadcasting our wavelength back to us. We have a natural and healthy tendency (besides when there is an "imp of the perverse") to gravitate towards those who feel good about themselves and radiate goodness, and to stay away from those who radiate the opposite. This paradigm is also true in our relationship with HaKadosh Baruch Hu, as it were, our *Tzeil* / 'Shadow'.

"Know what is Above you," instructs the Mishnah (*Avos*, 2:1). This is interpreted to mean, 'Know that all that exists Above is *from* you' (*Tzavaas haRivash,* 142. See also, *Nefesh haChayim*, 1:4, Note). In other words, we are to a great extent the creators of the reality we live in, and in a sense we create even that which comes from Above. We therefore draw to ourselves what we project outward, like an existential boomerang. We achieve what we believe, whether for the positive or for the negative. If we believe the ceiling is only so high, we will never strive to reach beyond it.

However, if we actively cultivate a positive and Bitachon-filled outlook on life, we will find that, generally speaking, things will work out. At the very least our consciousness will be deeply positive, which will in effect impact our experience of whatever we are going through. This in itself is a form of revelation and redemption.

Sometimes our outer, objective reality will not change for the better, no matter how strongly we think positive thoughts. Yet, we can bear in mind that 'objective' reality in itself has no definition or meaning; it is neither good nor bad, it just *is*. There are no objectively negative conditions. Negativity only exists subjectively, within the realm of our consciousness and evaluation, in our world of desire and expectation, disappointment and frustration. Life itself just is, and it is we who overlay it with definitions and context. And thus, on the deepest level, *Da'as* / awareness is everything, and the more we choose to overlay reality with a redemptive, positive, life-affirming paradigm, the more we can see goodness and redemption in the world, and the more we will then experience such goodness and light.

Lacking Bitachon and maintaining negative expectations of life makes an individual more vulnerable to hardship; perhaps not to its objective circumstances, but to its power to shake or break us. Certainly, to the extent that we dwell on the negative and wallow in our sorrow, our suffering and anguish will continue to cling to us and linger longer than necessary. It would do us well to always remember, טראכט גוט וועט זיין גוט / "Think good and it *will* be good." This is the level of Bitachon that the Baal Shem Tov revealed: active Bitachon actually draws down Chesed. The more Bitachon, the more goodness. On this level, it is up to you. And this, as we will see, is the essence of the month of Kislev and the Holy Days of Chanukah.

As the Baal Shem Tov teaches, even if a person deserves (for the purpose of cleansing his soul and reorienting him towards a proper path) to receive a judgement or harsh decree, through Bitachon the attribute of *Din* / judgment cannot take hold of him (*Keser Shem Tov*). It is as if he is protected by 'angels' from all negative forces and nothing can move or sway them from his defense (*Toldos Yaakov Yoseph*, Miketz), as King David says, שיר המעלות הבטחים בה כהר־ציון לא־ימוט לעולם ישב / "A song of ascents, those who trust in Hashem are like Mount Zion that cannot be moved, enduring forever" (*Tehilim*, 125:1). In a sense, such Bitachon is a kind of *Magen David* / Shield of David, a spiritual force field protecting one from their accusers and judgments.

The Mishnah says, הצועק לשעבר, הרי זו תפלת שוא... היה בא בדרך ושמע קול צווחה בעיר, ואמר יהי רצון שלא יהיו אלו בני ביתי, הרי זו תפלת שוא / "One who cries over the past, behold this is a vain prayer. How so? If he is coming home from a journey and he hears a cry of distress in the town and says, 'May it be His will that this is not from my house,' this is a vain prayer" (Mishnah, *Berachos*, 9:3). In other words, once there is a reality in the world we should no longer pray, as we cannot change what already is (*Berachos*, 60a. Although, see *Yerushalmi*, with regards to a woman about to give birth, אף היושב על המשבר יכול להשתנות: *Berachos*, 9:3). Yet, the Gemara tells us, מעשה בהלל הזקן שהיה בא בדרך ושמע קול צוחה בעיר אמר **מובטח** אני שאין זה בתוך ביתי ועליו הכתוב אומר משמועה רעה לא יירא נכון לבו **בטח** בה' / "There was an incident involving Hillel the Elder, who was coming on the road when he heard a scream in the city. He said, 'I am *certain* that the scream is not coming from my house.' And of him, the verse says, 'He shall not be afraid of evil tidings: his heart is steadfast, *trusting* in Hashem'" (*Tehilim*, 112:7).

This is a very deep level of Bitachon; Hillel had such overwhelming Bitachon in Hashem's goodness that he was able to declare מובטח אני / '*I am certain*', without the slightest bit of worry that he would be embarrassed by being disproved (*Ben Yehoyada*, Beitzah, 16a). The point of the story is that such a level of Bitachon is possible and that we should aspire to cultivate our ability to affirm with utter conviction that 'Hashem shows me *only* kindness and revealed goodness.'

An obvious question is, where does this conviction come from? Perhaps we deserve some measure of cleansing chastisement or 'unrevealed goodness' to help us learn a lesson, to correct our path or get us to a better place, and so forth? There is a defined system of cause and effect, action and reaction, otherwise called reward and punishment, so how can we be so certain or even aspire to imagine that Hashem should always surround us with revealed goodness? The great Spanish 15th Century philosopher, Rav Yoseph Albo, of the last generation of *Rishonim* / early Rabbis, writes in his magnum opus, *Sefer haIkarim* / 'Book of Fundamentals', והבוטח בה׳ חסד יסובבנהו, כלומר אף אם אינו ראוי מצד עצמו מדרך הבטחון להמשיך חסד חנם על הבוטחים בשם / "'But he who trusts in Hashem shall be surrounded with goodness' — this means that even if he is not worthy because of his actions, the nature of Bitachon is to draw down undeserved Chesed upon those who have Bitachon in Hashem" (*Sefer haIkarim*, 4:46). In other words, even if one is not deserving, in fact, even if one is a *Rasha* / debased person, Bitachon supports their claim, as the Medrash says, אפילו רשע ובוטח בה' חסד יסובבנו / "Even a Rasha who has Bitachon in Hashem, Chesed will surround him" (*Yalkut Shimoni*, Nach, 719).

This is the nature of Bitachon in HaKadosh Baruch Hu, and it is the way Hashem interacts with us and the world: when we focus on the goodness of Hashem and His Creation, and have trust in this goodness, we draw down and attract our proverbial "shadow", illuminating and revealing the goodness that surrounds us.

On a deeper level, through the act and mindset of fulfilling the Mitzvah of Bitachon, this in itself lifts us up to a place of *Zechus* / merit, and this becomes the *Kli* / vessel within which the goodness of Hashem becomes manifest and revealed to us. In this way, the more Bitachon we have, the more merit we attain, and the more Chesed we draw towards us, and in fact into the world at large.

THE MORE BITACHON WE HAVE IN HASHEM'S GOODNESS, THE MORE GOODNESS IS REVEALED IN OUR LIVES AND IN THE WORLD

As discussed, Bitachon is a form of *Ohr Chozer* / reflected light. It is not passive 'optimism' in the Goodness of Hashem and His Creation, nor is it merely a conviction that our life and the world will shift for the better on their own. Bitachon is an empowered state of mind, heart and action, in which we realize that "the Nature of the Ultimate Good is to bestow goodness." As a result of this realization, we sense that the world will eventually reach *Yom sheKulo Tov* / the Day of Only Good, and that we can move it along in this direction through our conscious input. Indeed, there is an inherent undercurrent in the world progressing toward goodness and Redemption, and we can tap into and amplify this awesome power. From this perspective, we can actively make positive changes in our lives and in the world, even at this very moment.

While Bitachon does begin with a positive inner conviction that things can be different, Bitachon also implies that our conviction will shine forth as action. We ourselves must set positive change in motion, in both our mind and our body, and this starts with making changes within our own selves and our personal lives.

"One good deed can tip the entire scale of the world towards goodness" (*Kiddushin*, 40a. Rambam, *Hilchos Teshuvah*, 3:4). As we are filled with Bitachon, hope, positivity, possibility and optimism, the world around us begins to also be infused with the same sense. Our personal Bitachon affects the world around us by spiritual osmosis, replacing despair, hopelessness, negativity and pessimism with the potential for goodness to reveal itself. Today we understand that measuring a subatomic particle in one location may instantaneously affect the measurement of another particle thousands of miles away. This is referred to as 'quantum entanglement'. Two particles that have been in contact become deeply 'entangled' or interconnected. When they are then separated, they can 'communicate' faster than light, a change in one prompting a virtually simultaneous change in the other. This phenomenon does not diminish with distance. Such 'quantum non-locality' has been tested experimentally for more than 25 years. The amazing ability of birds to locate their home from thousands of miles away may be associated with non-local quantum phenomena. Regardless of the authority of ever-changing science, this idea can serve as a good *Mashal* / metaphor or example, and help us understand the phenomenon of our consciousness affecting the consciousness of the entire world.

The ability to live with the knowledge that "The nature of the Good is to bestow goodness," and that there will be a יום שכולו טוב / *Yom sheKulo Tov* / a time when all is good, is a unique privilege and potential revealed within human beings. HaKadosh Baruch Hu continually observes Creation, as if from the outside, and says, '*Tov* / it is good, and it is moving towards the Ultimate Good.' We can, and must, put on the Creator's proverbial lenses and see the good of Creation. The more actively we focus on and emphasize the good in the world, the more goodness will be revealed in the world, for 'the observer affects the observed,' and even Chesed from Above "is from you".

THE 36 HIDDEN LIGHTS

The word כסלו / *Kislev* can be divided into two parts: כס / *Kis(ui)* / 'hidden', and לו / the letters Lamed-Vav, numerically meaning '36'. The 'Hidden 36' refers to the *Ohr haGanuz* / the 'Hidden Light' of Gan Eden, which is the goodness, perfection and *Yichud* / oneness that was first revealed in the primordial Garden and then hidden away for the Future יום שכולו טוב / Day of Only Good. But what does this Hidden Light have to do with the number 36?

According to Chazal, Adam and Chavah spent 36 hours in Gan Eden before they were exiled as a result of eating from the Tree of Dualistic Knowledge: 12 hours of Friday, plus the 24 hours of Shabbos. These 36 hours were filled with Divine light. With it they were able to see from one end of the world to the other. Once Shabbos was over, however, this light was hidden as Adam and Chavah were thrust out into the darkness of the world, and thus it is called "the Hidden Light" (*Medrash Rabbah*, Bereishis, 12:6. See also Yerushalmi, *Berachos*, 8:5). This Divine light was imprinted within human consciousness on the deepest level, and will one day shine forth again once we return to the Garden, so to speak, and reconnect to the Tree of Life.

Gan Eden is the 'garden' of Unity, the world of the Tree of Life. Adam and Chavah lived in this paradisiacal consciousness for 36 luminous hours on the day they were created and on their first Shabbos; their very existence is thus rooted in this state. And we are each a part of their inclusive soul which is known as *Adam Kadmon* / Original Human Being, and therefore our own primordial state is also bathed in and permeated by the Ohr haGanuz. We were formed and founded within Gan Eden; the Ohr haGanuz is where we come from, and where we are ultimately headed toward. It is our original identity, our native land, our foundation and our destiny.

After Adam and Chavah ate from the Tree of Knowledge and essentially disconnected and separated themselves from Gan Eden and the Tree of Life world-view, Hashem asked Adam: איכה / *Ayekah* / Where are you? This question was not only an expression of compassion, nor was it only a subtle teaching on the appropriate way to initiate a meaningful conversation. It was also an existential question: "Where are you in this situation? Are you present?"

Significantly, the word Ayekah's numerical value is 36 (*Medrash Zuta*, Eichah, 1:1). And so the question is also: "Where are your 36 lights? What have you done with your illuminating essence? Where is your deepest identity, the root of your being? You had the highest, deepest *Ohr* / light in the universe, a light through which you could observe all of reality and behold the unity within all Creation, 'from one end of the world to the next,' and you chose to identify as *something* apart from the *everything* and enter the world of separation, dissension, conflict, and fragmented multiplicity. My precious child, if you can realize 'where' you now are in all of this, and how you got there, you will not be lost and you can return to where you belong!"

This thirty-six hours of basking in Divine light and seeing from one end of the world to the other was enough exposure as to be unforgettable, to create a homing instinct that would eventually guide all souls back to their origin. Therefore, when the primordial humans ate from the Tree of Knowledge, they already retained an indelible imprint and memory of this Light, which was then hidden within the Torah for all future generations to rediscover and reintegrate in awareness, thought, word and deed. In fact, Rav Eliezer of Worms points out that 36 is the number of times the word *Ohr* / light appears in the *Chumash* / Five Books of Moshe (*Sefer Rokeach*).

Related to this complex of ideas is the teaching that in every generation there are 36 *Tzadikim Nistarim* / Hidden Tzadikim present in the world who work to sustain, nurture and guard the primordial light hidden with Creation (*Sukkos*, 52b). Concealed, unassuming, and virtually unknown, these 36 righteous souls are completely attuned to the Ohr haGanuz that still shines in Gan Eden and deep within themselves. They consciously know that this is their place of origin, as they have rediscovered and reintegrated it in their deep engagement with all aspects of the Torah, including its *Nistar* / hidden dimension. They are thus able to kindle this light, even within the darkness of exile, and even to illuminate other people and situations with its Divine glow. (The fullness of Torah is called *PaRDeS* / Paradise, a four-letter acronym for the dimensions of ***Peshat*** / Simple Meaning, such as Tanach in itself; ***Remez*** / Hinted Meaning, such as parts of practical laws and their sources; ***Drush*** / Interpretation, such as Medrashic explanations; and ***Sod*** / Secret or hidden teachings, such as Kabbalistic wisdom. There is also an inclusive fifth dimension of Torah which openly and generously reveals the Light of Paradise 'hidden' within all these four dimensions, as well as within the world itself. This essential teaching is called *Chassidus* / Open Generosity.)

This dynamic of great light emerging from relative obscurity is expressed in myriad ways throughout the Torah. For instance, it says: ויהי־ערב ויהי־בקר / "And it was evening and it was morning...." In Torah Law a day begins with the night; in other words, light begins in darkness. "Night" in Hebrew is ערב / *Erev*, which is numerically 272. "Morning" is בקר / *Boker* (when spelled as read it could include a Vav: בוקר) which numerically is 308. The numerical difference between 272 and 308 is 36. Thus, the number 36 alludes to the 'hidden' dimension that separates night from day, the liminal space that allows the transition from darkness to light.

For 36 hours the Light of Creation enabled Adam and Chavah to see from one end of the world to the other, because there was no separation in space or between 'opposites' such as night and day. Erev and Boker were both enfolded within the Oneness of Reality. In the world of the Tree of Knowledge, the world of separation, there is one place as opposed to another place, and they are separated from each other by varying degrees of distance. There is day and light, and there is night and darkness, and they are isolated from each other. In the world of the Tree of Life, of Gan Eden, of the Higher Light, there is only One, even as It is refracted and reflected into 'the many'. Here, 'the many' openly senses and reveals the One, and there is no substantial separation. It is the inclusion of multiplicity within Unity, the enfolding of darkness within a context of Endless Light.

It is important to distinguish the difference between this primordial light and the celestial and physical lights we are accustomed to seeing in nature. On *Yom Echad* / Day One of Creation, Hashem said, "Let there be Light, and there was light." The functioning sun and moon, by which living entities perceive physical light, were only fashioned on Day Four of Creation. In the Day 'One' reality, the unified, singular Day of Creation, all that existed was *Ohr*, the higher Light of Unity that precedes and includes night and day, 'here' and 'there', one entity and another. In short: physical light separates one thing from another, while spiritual light unifies all as one.

It is also important to note that such Higher Light is not in the aspect of 'fire'. Whereas fire, in order to exist, needs to cancel out another entity such as a wick or oil, the Higher Light does not extinguish any 'other' in order to exist, rather It embraces and includes all entities integrally and non-separately. Moshe experiences this Ohr haGanuz when he sees that "the bush was on fire but was not consumed," as will be explored later on. This reality of Infinite Light is our deepest, most hidden and primordial state. It is our inherent birthright, which is more revealed and accessible during this month of כסלו / Kislev, and especially during Chanukah, as will be explored.

And yet, we must ask, why are these '36 lights' hidden? Our sages tell us that they are hidden for the righteous in the future (*Chagigah*, 12a). And where are they hidden? Says the Baal Shem Tov, they are hidden in the Torah (*Degel Machaneh Ephraim*, Bereishis. *Yosher Divrei Emes*, 3. See also, *Nefesh HaChayim*, end of Sha'ar 1, Haga'ah. Note, *Zohar* 1, p, 264a. Medrash *Tanchumah*, Noach). In every generation, through our full engagement and participation in Torah we reveal this higher light (*Zohar* 2, 148b). The deeper we dig within, the more of the self is involved with the Torah; and the deeper we excavate within the Torah itself, the more connected we become with the Ohr haGanuz within it and within ourselves.

Although the Torah is one, it can be seen as having two dimensions, two 'lights'. There is a revealed aspect of the Torah, the Written Torah, the prophetic revelation. We are mere recipients of this revelation, which is referred to as *Ohr Yashar* / Direct Light. And there is an oral aspect of Torah, the *Ohr Chozer* / Reflected Light of Torah. This is revealed specifically through our human interaction with sacred texts, our intellectual engagement in deciphering, contemplating and using all our unique faculties and ways of thinking in Torah study.

Direct light is analogous to walking into a dark room and switching on the lights. Immediately, the room becomes illuminated and everything in the room is clear. You can see where the table is and where the chair is. Reflected Light is more similar to walking into a dark room and standing in the darkness for a while until your eyes get used to the dark, and you can start to deduce where the table is situated and where the chair is in relation to it. The written Torah is the 'Direct Light' from Above clearly illuminating what should and should not be done. The oral aspects of Torah are 'Reflected Light', and these take a lot more time and exertion to bring one to clarity, demanding our full participation with the text in order to truly understand what we are learning, rather than merely reading the words (whereas one who reads the Written Torah without any understanding, has fulfilled the Mitzvah of Talmud Torah: Alter Rebbe, *Hilchos Talmud Torah*, 2:12-13. See also *Pesach Einayim* on *Avodah Zarah*, 19a. Hakdama, *Emes l'Yaakov*). The hidden lights of Gan Eden are more concentrated within the Oral Torah. The entire oral dimension of Torah is codified in the Talmud, known as the Gemara. Appropriately, there are 36 tractates of the Babylonian Gemara reflecting the 36 Lights of the Ohr haGanuz.

The meanings of the words and arguments of the Gemara often seem difficult, unclear, 'dark' or opaque. The entire mode of Talmudic dialogue is in the form of question and answer, counter-question, resolution, and then deeper questions. Often, despite the constant debates and counter debates, no resolution is reached. However, the Oral Torah is 'revealed' through this very dialectical tension. A kind of light and redemption is discovered through the arduous labor of questioning, and settling into 'darkness' and exile. Our sages tell us that the verse, במחשכים הושיבני כמתי עולם / "He placed me in darkness, like those long dead" (*Eichah* 3:6), refers to the Talmud of *Bavel* / Babylon (*Sanhedrin*, 24a. The sages of Bavel are connected to 'darkness' *Zevachim*, 60b. Ritvah, *Yuma*, 57a, and (perhaps) a light that comes from the darkness). In Talmudic learning, clarity and wisdom, light and resolution are attained, but only commensurate with the toil of questioning and debate. העם ההלכים בחשך ראו אור גדול / "The people that walk in darkness have seen a great light" (*Yeshayahu*, 9:1). The "people" referred to in this verse are the masters of the Gemara, "who beheld a great light when the Holy One, blessed be He, enlightened them as to what is prohibited and permitted, pure and impure" (*Tanchuma*, Noach 3). This is the light of the Ohr haGanuz, the hidden 36 Lights of Gan Eden that are tucked away in the 36 volumes of the Gemara, which are revealed only when we engage them, dig into ourselves and reveal our own inner Light through the prism of Torah.

Within the Written Torah itself, the origin of the Oral Torah is when Moshe explained the Torah to the Children of Israel, and translated the Torah into the 70 languages of the world, so that all could understand. This is the meaning of the verse, "It was in the fortieth year, on the first day of the Eleventh Month (the first day of Shevat…) הואיל משה באר את־התורה / "Moshe began to explain this Torah" (*Devarim,* 1:3-5). 'This means Moshe explained to them the Torah in 70 languages — and he began doing so on Rosh Chodesh Shevat' (*Sotah*, 32a. *Tanchuma*, Devarim, 2:1. Rashi, ad loc). The *Seder Olam* has an amazing insight regarding this time period of Moshe translating the Torah. Moshe was translating the Torah from the first day of Shevat, and since he passed away on the Seventh of Adar, we could assume that he continued translating throughout the sixth of Adar, meaning that in total he translated the Torah for 36 days. In this way, Moshe was initiating the Oral Torah for precisely 36 days (*Seder Olam,* 10). For 36 days Moshe transmitted the kernels of the oral aspect of the Torah, and today these kernels are represented by the 36 *Mesechtos* / tractates of Gemara (corresponding to the 36 lights kindled on Chanukah. Rebbe Pinchas of Koritz, *Medrash Pinchas*).

Chanukah & the 36 Lights

In Hebrew, כס / *Kis*, the first part of the word Kislev, also means 'pocket'. The same letters can be pronounced as כוס / *Kos*, meaning 'cup'. In this context, כסלו / *Kislev* means the 'pocket' or 'cup' — the vessel — that holds the ל"ו / Lamed-Vav, the 36 lights. During this month of *Ohr Chozer* / reflected light we have extra *Koach* / power to reveal the 36 Hidden Lights by kindling the cumulative 36 lights in the 'vessel' of our Chanukah Menorah.

Chanukah begins on the 25th day of Kislev. Indeed, the 25th word in the Torah is *Ohr* / light, referring to the Ohr haGanuz from the First Day of Creation: "And Hashem said, יהי אור / *Yehi Ohr* / 'Let there be light'" (*Bereishis,* 1:3). Additionally, the word before *Ohr* is יהי / *Yehi* / "Let there be..." which is numerically 25 (*Shaloh*, Torah she-b'Ksav, Tzon Yoseph, 12). The Ohr haGanuz seems to be saying, 'Kindle me and draw down my אור on the 25th of the month by beginning to kindle the 36 lights of the Menorah.'

On the 25th day of Elul the world was created, Day One of Creation, so to speak. On this day, Hashem said "Let there be light," and the Ohr of Creation was revealed. Exactly nine months prior to the 25th of Elul is the 25th of Kislev, the first night of Chanukah. Nine months "before" Day One, the Ohr is 'conceived' in the Divine mind, as it were. In other words, on the 25th of Kislev the first glimmer of the idea arose, hidden within the Creator, to 'give birth' to the Light of *Yehi Ohr*. Millenia later, on this very night, a glimmer of the Ohr began to be revealed within the 'hiddenness' of the darkness of history and the darkest season, by means of the miracle of Chanukah, as it was perceived in the minds of the Tzadikim who were engaging in the Oral Torah. We too reveal this glimmer of the Ohr haGanuz when we kindle our Menorahs beginning on the 25th of Kislev.

Ohr is also connected to the Chassidic Yom Tov in Kislev, *Yud-Tes Kislev* / the 19th of Kislev. This day is referred to by the Rebbe Rashab (Rebbe Shalom DovBer of Chabad) as "the Rosh Hashanah of Chassidus", and "the day when our אור וחיות / light and vitality is given to us" (*Hayom Yom*, Yud-Tes Kislev).

On Yud-Tes Kislev the Alter Rebbe, Rebbe שניאור / *Schneur* (שני / *Shnei* / two, אור / *Ohr* / lights) Zalman, was released from prison after being falsely charged with treason, and after having to defend the teachings of Chassidus, the distilled essence of the Oral Torah, and the path of the Baal Shem Tov and his students.

In the fall of 1798, the Alter Rebbe was charged for treason on the grounds that — besides his collecting monies for the poor in *Eretz Yisrael* / Israel, which was then under the Ottoman Empire, a sworn enemy of Russia — his teachings, the teachings of Chassidus, were not a recognized practice of traditional Judaism and thus were a threat to the prevailing authority structures. The Alter Rebbe was interrogated for many weeks, and was forced to explain some of the basic tenets of Judaism and various details of Chassidus and its practices, for example the emphasis on prayer. On the 19th of Kislev he was released. The Alter Rebbe saw his arrest and eventual release as Divine signs. Being that the charges were related to the teaching and spreading of Chassidus, the teachings of the Baal Shem Tov and his teacher, the Maggid of Mezritch, he interpreted the arrest as a Heavenly indictment against the revealing of Chassidus. Likewise, his release on the 19th of Kislev was a confirmation and vindication of the importance of teaching Chassidus. In fact, on a certain 19th of Kislev many years prior, his Rebbe, the Maggid, passed away and told him before he passed: "This day is our Yom Tov."

As hinted in his name, *Shnei-Ohr,* the path of Chassidus is the path of light (*She'eiris Yisrael* [Vilednick] p. 152). It rooted in the deepest Ohr, that which was "hidden away for the future". This light can overwhelm the darkness of one's inner psyche by kindling the soul's power of illumination (Rebbe Rayatz, *Igros Kodesh,* 3. p 547).

Chassidus is, in fact, a *Shnei* / 'double' Ohr: it works both to counter the darkness of our internal and external exiles, and to reveal a glimmer of the light of *Olam haBa* / the world to come.

SENSE

THE CONVENTIONAL WORLD IDENTIFIES FIVE SENSES, while Sefer Yetzirah speaks of twelve *Chushim* / senses. In addition to the more commonly understood definition of 'senses', the word *Chush* can also mean, 'a sensitive level of perception, understanding, appreciation and 'skill' in relation to a specific psycho-spiritual process or function. For example, a 'sense of sleep' is a deep understanding and appreciation of sleep, including what sleep represents spiritually, as well as the practical skills and abilities that make one's experience of sleep both peaceful and beneficial. (Indeed, the definition of 'sleep' can also include preparations for sleep, in the words of Rashi, דאית ליה בשכבך כל זמן שבני אדם עוסקין לילך ולשכב / "(according to Rebbe Eliezer) who maintains that 'when you sleep' refers to the entire time that people are busy going to sleep: Rashi, *Berachos*, 4a).

These twelve *Chushim* are also the twelve activities that the Torah describes the Creator performing in the perpetual process of maintaining the world (*Pirush haRaavad, Sefer Yetzirah*). As we are created in the Divine image we also possess all twelve Chushim, at least in potential.* Every month gives us the ability and strength to expand our vessels (potentials) for a particular *Chush*, along with its corresponding Divine Attributes. When we align and refine our consciousness via these *Chushim*, we can harness the qualities of each month in a most profound and meaningful way.

According to *Sefer Yetzirah*, the *Chush* / sense connected with Kislev is sleep. Perhaps the meta-physical sleepy nature of this month is reflected in the world of nature and the condition of the Northern Hemisphere during this time. In general, the world is more asleep in Kislev. In the animal kingdom, many species of animals are hibernating throughout Kislev. In the vegetative kingdom, most trees seem to be 'falling asleep' as they release their leaves and cease to show outward life and growth. Even the days themselves seem to be falling asleep, as they become shorter and darker, until around the end of the month. During Kislev, the world itself seems to be sleeping.

RAIN AND SLEEP

Kislev is a continuation of the rainy season, begun in Cheshvan, the previous month. When it is rainy, or for that matter snowy,

* Even if one is blind, for example, he always has the *potential* for sight — it's just that he is currently missing the physical vessels (capacities) for it: *Pirush haGra*, Hakdamah, Sefer Yetzirah. However, the sense of sight is included in the person's Divine image, as it were. Obviously, a physically blind person could have immense vessels for spiritual sight.

people generally become more tired and sleepy. This apparently stems from patterns formed during the millennia when it was common for people to work the land. When the weather of this season prevented physical labor in the fields, our predecessors were forced to rest. There is a type of genetically encoded 'memory' provoked when it rains, telling the body to go to sleep. Yet, on a more meta-physical, inner level, as the *Sod Yesharim* explains, this sleepiness is Hashem 'talking' to us, saying, 'My dear children, you have done your part; you have plowed the land and worked hard tilling and pruning. Now it is time for Me to do My job and bring rain to the fields. I will take care of the world and you can sleep peacefully.'

When it rained and the people were forced to stop working, they were compelled to relinquish control over the land, and confirm their dependency upon the rains for their success. Those who were more spiritually sensitive became acutely aware that the rains, and in turn their life and livelihood, were in the hands of the Creator of All Life. This *Bitachon* / ultimate trust in Hashem allowed them to put down their plowshares and peacefully relax or even fall asleep, even when their future harvest was uncertain and out of their hands.

Even today, people are naturally more sleepy when it is rainy outside, this is part of our in-built reflex of trust in our Creator. When it is raining Hashem is saying to us, 'Even if you do not own or work in the fields, now you can take a rest and trust in the fact that I am the ultimate Master and everything is in 'My Hands'. You can rest with ease.'

BITACHON: THE EASE AND PEACEFULNESS OF SLEEP

It is interesting that Sefer Yetzirah puts sleep in the same general category as the senses of smell and sight. What does this mean? Most people have a utilitarian relationship with sleep: they sleep because they are exhausted or they seek an escape from the waking state. According to the Gemara, a human being cannot go for three days without sleep (*Nedarim*, 15a). This is what we call instinctual, utilitarian sleep. Some, however, have a *Chush* — a refined sense or taste for the 'art' of sleep. Some people simply drop into bed at night, but others understand sleep as a skill, art or ritual, demanding intentional preparations, breathing or visualization techniques, special pillows, custom mattresses, fine linen, and so forth. It could be seen as a waste of time to focus excessively on sleeping or to indulge in over-sleeping, which serves no real purpose and does not even make one feel more rested. Yet, there is an element of peacefulness even in these kinds of sleep, and peacefulness shows trust.

Resting with ease, pleasantness and peacefulness is the real Chush of sleep.

Everyone, and in fact everything, in the world needs sleep: animals, trees, and even the oceans, as Rebbe Pinchas of Koritz teaches (*Imrei Pinchas,* Seder Hayom, 215). Just as humans and animals sleep, so does all of nature. A tree in the winter is 'sleeping', and the ocean when it is placid is 'sleeping'. This is all part of the utilitarian aspect of sleep, which is primarily for the purpose of gaining strength in the future. The Chush of sleep, however, is the ability to sleep with a deep sense of faith and trust. An adept sleeper has deeper trust in Divine support and protection, and can thus rest peacefully, as the

Book of *Mishlei* / Proverbs says: ...אם־תשכב לא־תפחד ושכבת וערבה שנתך כי ה יהיה בכסלך / "If you will rest you will not worry, you will lay down and your sleep will be pleasant...for Hashem will be כסלך / your trust" (*Mishlei*, 3:24-26). If we put our כסל / trust (which is the root word of *Kislev*) in Hashem, we will lay down peacefully and our sleep will be pleasant, restful and refreshing.

Sleep is "1/60th of death" (*Berachos*, 57b. *Medrash Rabbah*, Bereishis, 17:5). 'Surrender' is a central ingredient to sleeping peacefully, because as we relax into sleep we must release our control over our environment and our ability to respond to it. A person needs to allow himself to 'die' a little, to relinquish all personal authority, and even survival instincts, in order to slip into the 'nothingness' of sleep.

For certain people this form of surrender is frightening and they have difficulty falling asleep. When we are awake we are in our egoic self-preservation state, always on the look-out for real or imagined danger. To sleep is to surrender the ego, to let the self slip into the depths of the subconscious. For this reason, many children have a hard time falling asleep, because they are very much inhabiting their egoic narrative. This is appropriate, as building an ego is necessary and healthy for children. They do not want to 'miss out' on life and do not want to surrender their awareness. Positive human development moves from pre-personal/infancy, to personal/childhood, to trans-personal/adulthood to integral/maturity. Many people who are stuck in a child-like paradigm have a hard time surrendering themselves in sleep. Yet, as the Pasuk above tells us, if you have more *Bitachon* / trust in Hashem, you will worry less and you will be able to lay down and sleep more peacefully.

A common malaise is insomnia, an inability to fall asleep or to stay asleep throughout the night. Obviously, one suffering from insomnia does not feel refreshed and restored upon awakening, and this lack of quality sleep can hinder their full capacity to function during the waking hours. Chronic insomnia can lead to all types of serious health problems. While most do not experience 'chronic insomnia', many people do experience some form of anxiety and worry, affecting their ability to fall or stay asleep — either somewhat regularly, or at least during particularly stressful times.

Considering all the issues that can contribute to an inability to fall asleep, including physical discomfort, noise, eating too close to bedtime, and room temperature, the dominant reason why people suffer from an inability to sleep is self-generated worry and anxiety. Sometimes there is even a primal anxiety that one will not rise, G-d forbid, in the morning. Without Bitachon, worry has free reign; one's mind is occupied with self-centered doubts, unresolved conflicts, fears about the unknown future, or simply unfinished business from the prior day. As one is about to fall asleep the mind races from one issue to the next, impeding the restful quietness of mind required to temporarily relinquish control over one's life and simply fall asleep.

Clearly, to rectify our Chush of sleep and recover its ערבה / pleasantness and refreshment, we must refine our faculty of Bitachon and establish an awareness that our lives are ultimately in the hands of the All-Loving, Good and Generous Creator. To have trust is to know how to let go. The Rebbe Rashab of Chabad once said that an individual who is able to fall asleep easily also has an easier time dropping into a calm, relaxed state for *Davennen* / prayer. Similar to sleep, before we Daven we need to let go of all our other involvements and activities. In the morning, we need to put aside our thoughts and anxieties regarding the upcoming day. In the middle of the day, with the *Minchah* / afternoon prayers, we may have to let go of even more intense connections to our ongoing activities, and in the evening after work we may need to release ourselves from the incessant to-do list of unfinished tasks and responsibilities. In every case, we need to let go of distractions and complications in order to enter into a meditative state of intentionality and pure presence in the moment.

When we recite praises we have to allow ourselves to be emotionally open. When we cover our eyes to say the Shema and when we place our feet together in the *Amida* / standing silent prayer, we have to let down our guard and enter a spiritual world, trusting that Hashem will watch over us. Bitachon is essential to prayer. Many even have a custom to recite the verse, ה׳ צבאות אשרי אדם בטח בך / "Hashem of Hosts, happy is the man who trusts in You" (*Tehilim*, 85:13) three times before entering each of the three prayers of the day. This kind of pronouncement entrains one to relax and release oneself fully into Hashem's care and presence. In this way, sleep is similar to prayer; to sleep well we need to have the Bitachon to let down our guard and relax our minds and bodies. And like prayer, many people recite or repeat certain phrases or passages to themselves as a preparatory practice before going to sleep.

In truth, even when the root of the insomnia is chemical or physiological and medication is required, Bitachon is extremely helpful as well. Your mindset affects your neurochemistry. Stressful thinking produces certain chemical reactions in one's body. Positive calming thoughts produce another set of chemical reactions that amplify those energies, transmuting those thoughts into feelings and even physical sensations. Through resolute Bitachon we can form new neural pathways that will be supportive and conducive for sleep.

Sometimes, to have even basic Bitachon is a challenge. In various circumstances, people can feel stuck in their worries, doubts, uncertainties, and narrowness of perception, making it difficult to be optimistic and have trust in the Presence and Goodness of Hashem. And so, the prophet declares, בטחו בה עדי עד / *Bitchu b'Hashem Adei Ad* / "Trust in Hashem, forever and ever" (*Yeshayahu*, 26:4). בטחון / trust, in numerical value (Beis/2, Tes/9, Ches/8, Vav/6, Nun/50) is 75. The word עד, plus 1 representing the word itself, is also 75. Thus the verse means, 'Trust in Hashem *Adei Ad* / until you attain עד, trust." Sometimes we need to consciously project Bitachon in our thoughts in order to actually feel Bitachon in our hearts and bodies. This is another example of the Chasidic saying we discussed earlier: "Think good, and it will be good."

YAAKOV SLEEPING

As mentioned, Yaakov was buried during Kislev. Yaakov "did not die" (*Ta'anis*, 5b); we could therefore suggest, poetically, that he is just 'sleeping'. His immortality, as well as his peaceful sleep, are symbolic of the collective Bitachon of the People of Israel in their future and in their ultimate 'awakening' in *Techiyas haMeisim* / the Resurrection of the Dead — the reanimation of everything of value from the past and its revelation in the present.

♈

SIGN

EACH MONTH CONTAINS THE ZODIAC INFLUENCE OF A particular constellation, referred to in Hebrew as a *Mazal.* A constellation is a perceivably patterned grouping of visible stars. Today we count 88 constellations in the night sky. Out of all of these, one constellation is predominantly visible on the horizon at the beginning of each month.

Each constellation refracts the light of the cosmos differently, alternately reflecting times that are more conducive to war and times that are more conducive for the flourishing of peace, for example (*Yalkut Reuveini*, Bereishis, Os 56). The *Zohar* teaches that each sign can manifest positively or negatively (*Zohar* 3, 282a). In this way, the constellations can have either a productive or a destructive influence in one's life. However, it is not the cluster of stars that have any real influence, rather, the formation in the sky is an external expression of how HaKadosh Baruch Hu is, *Kaviyachol* / if you will, interacting with Creation at that moment.

It is important to keep in mind that whether our proclivities are innate or 'celestially influenced', we still possess the free choice of response to any situation that arises in our life. We have the ability to choose our reaction to what has been projected onto us, including the qualities of a certain Mazal. For example, a person born under the influence of Mars, 'the Red Planet', may have a tendency to be involved with 'blood', but he or she also has the ability to employ this inherent tendency for good or ill. Such a person could choose to be a violent criminal or a life-saving surgeon.

Due to the prevailing popular belief that the stars exert a fatalistic influence upon world history and human development, we need to repeatedly emphasize that anyone can rise above these influences altogether and be unaffected by them. Despite all the forces and influences in our life — physical and psychological conditions, upbringing, education, environment, financial status, etc. — we always have the freedom to choose. We have the choice to live as either the *effect* of our conditions (as passive receivers of what life serves us), or as the *cause* of what comes next, thereby becoming proactive co-creators of our lives. When we begin to live more proactively, the influences of our birth constellation and the Mazal of each month function less as positive or negative 'influences', and more as 'tools' that can help us climb ever higher into our freedom of being.

The astrological sign of Kislev is the קשת / *Keshes* / bow or *Kashos* / the Archer, also called Sagittarius. The mythological figure of Sagittarius is a centaur with a drawn bow. A drawn bow is a physical image of *Ohr Chozer* / Reflected Light. When the string and arrow are drawn back, a great tension is created. The bowman trusts, however, that this tension will allow the arrow to fly with power and focus when released. Sometimes a drawing back is necessary to move forward; sometimes a descent is necessary to bring a greater ascent. Darkness leads to light when it motivates us to ignite the lamp of our lives.

KESHES: SLEEP & THE RAINBOW

Pulling back or pressing down in order to catapult forward or upward is a theme related to the sense of the month, sleep. Going to sleep involves 'descending' into unconsciousness and psycho-physical vulnerability. When we awaken and arise, we are more refreshed and strengthened. Similarly, in a time of darkness, when we hold tenaciously to the sparks of our hopes and dreams, we can propel ourselves like an arrow to the greatest heights of illuminating revelation.

Keshes also means rainbow. A rainbow is also a form of 'reflected light', since it appears when sunlight reflects off mist in the air (Ramban, *Bereishis*, 9:13: ואנחנו על כרחנו נאמין לדברי היונים שמלהט השמש באויר הלח יהיה הקשת בתולדה כי בכלי מים לפני השמש יראה כמראה הקשת). Kislev is a rainy month, and in some countries rainbows are often seen during this time of the year.

It was in the month of Kislev when a rainbow first appeared to Noach as a sign of Hashem's covenant with humanity. The rains of the Great Flood had come down mostly in the month of Cheshvan. A year later, when the waters had subsided, Noach left the Ark on the 28th of Cheshvan, and the next day on the 29th he made offerings. Soon thereafter he heard the Divine promise: "I have set קשתי / My rainbow in the clouds, and it will be the sign of the covenant between Myself and the earth…I will remember My covenant…Never again will the waters become a flood" (*Bereishis*, 9:13-15). From this point forward, the day of Rosh Chodesh Kislev, the air was cleansed, as it were. From then on, a ray of sunlight that shines from Above to below could be seen reflected in the moisture as a rainbow, projecting the light back upwards.

Perhaps this is the reason that בחדש התשעי קראו צום / "In the ninth month (the people) declared a fast day" (*Yirmiyahu*, 36:9). Why? Because the act of fasting, which is meant to effect a shift in Heavenly judgments, is also an expression of Ohr Chozer. Our initiative and actions below are meant to be reflected in the Heavens, just like a rainbow. In fact, there is a manuscript version of Rashi's commentary that is older than the one most commonly referenced, which states that the day of Rosh Chodesh Kislev was like the day of Yom Kippur, a day of fasting and atonement. The quality of this day continues to resonate with hope and empowerment.

KESHES AS PRAYER

Keshes, the bow, is also related to prayer. The image of a Keshes is a half circle (*Eiruvin*, 55a), and a half circle depicts 'reaching' for completion, calling out for wholeness, as in to become a full circle. ***Keshes*** thus refers to the act of *Bakasha* / requesting, a modality of prayer.

Yaakov tells his beloved son Yoseph, "And now, I assign to you one portion more than to your brothers, which I wrested from the Amorites בחרבי ובקשתי / with my sword and bow" (*Bereishis*, 48:22). The traditional translator of the Torah, Unkelos, translates the words "which I have wrested from the Amorites בחרבי ובקשתי" as, "which I have wrested from the Amorites *with my prayer and pleading*" (Unkelos, ad loc. As the Gemara says, חרבי זו תפלה קשתי זו בקשה. *Baba Basra*, 123a). Prayer is an act of inner battle, for which we use a spiritual sword and bow. Our *Tefilah* / prayer reaches upwards like an arrow shot from a bow, and when it hits its target Above, it draws down new life force and blessings below.

One physical posture of Tefilah is clasping one's hands, the right hand over the left, and placing them both above the heart (see *Shabbos*, 10a). Rav Yehudah Chayit, the great Spanish 16th Century *Mekubal* / Kabbalist, writes that by placing both hands upon one's heart in prayer we are as if clasping a bow (*Pirush haChayit*, Ma'areches Elokus, 10. See also *Nefutzos Yehudah*, Derush 24). In this position, the hands can be imagined as pulling back the bow of our heart to shoot the arrows of our tongue, our prayers, into the heart of Heaven. When we pull back the bow of the heart, we can release the arrows, the words of our tongue, forward with the force of *Kavanah* / intentionality. In this way, our prayers are more likely to 'hit their mark', so to speak, and create an opening for *Shefa* / a downflow of blessing into our lives.

In general, Tefilah requires feeling the gravity of our lowliness and apparent distance from HaKadosh Baruch Hu, and then, like a drawn bow, catapulting ourselves to the highest of heights. The act of Tefilah is the recognition that we are only a 'half circle', and that we are in a state of *Cheser* / lack. The deeper we draw this 'half circle' inwards, and the more we are open and sensitive to our own darkness and state of exile, the more powerfully we can propel ourselves 'upward' toward completion and unity with the Source of all Life. In this way, Tefilah is a perfect expression of 'reflected light'. We ask and reach out for what we need, rather than receive it spontaneously from Above; we pull deeper 'downwards' to go higher 'upwards'.

Appropriately, Tefilah is also intricately related to Bitachon; it is the crucible within which we refine our trust in our own half-circle self, and our abilities to effect change in our lives and in the world. HaKadosh Baruch Hu created us like this, with all of our collective and individual lacks and needs, for a reason. He wants us to actively voice, articulate and develop our dreams, aspirations, hopes and longings. Tefilah is one of our primary mediums for co-creating the world in collaboration with Hashem. Tefilah is a space in which both our Bitachon in HaKadosh Baruch Hu, and in our own capacities, are solidified and strengthened. This is the epitome of Ohr Chozer.

As a reflection of Keshes, those who are born under this Mazal are filled with confidence and hope. Sagittarians are generally optimistic people and good friends. They love life and trust the dynamic of 'Reflected Light' — they feel that challenges bring bigger opportunities and greater resolve. They love to travel, are adventurous, and also have a burning desire to explore inner spiritual worlds. They are inclined to share their gained wisdom with whomever asks.

TRIBE

Every month of the year is connected with one of the Twelve Tribes of Israel, the sons of Yaakov (*Sefer Yetzirah*. Medrash, *Osyos Rebbe Akiva*, Dalet). The tribe associated with Kislev is Binyamin / Benjamin. Binyamin's original name is Ben Oni / Son of Sorrow/ he is initially characterized in the Torah as a product of darkness (*Bereishis*, 35:18) since his mother Rachel dies while giving birth to him. When Rachel is in labor, the Torah uses the term בהקשתה / she had difficulty in giving birth. This term has the same root as the word קשת / *Keshes* / bow, as Rachel's difficult labor was like a tensely drawn bow. Through drawing herself back into her pain, and deeply feeling her contractions of labor, she catapulted the life of a Tzadik, Binyamin, into this world. Eventually, through her passing on, her 'going to sleep', as it were (sleep being the sense of the month, and sleep or rest being associated with Binyamin, regarding whom it says, "...between the shoulders he rests": *Devarim*, 33:12. *Pirush haRaavad,* Sefer Yetzirah), she brought new life, a new future and a new Light into the world.

This new light that emerges out of the darkness of his birth circumstances and Rachel's death is renamed 'Binyamin', which means Son of *Yamin* / the South, referring to *Eretz Yisrael* / the Land of Israel. Hundreds of years later, after Binyamin's birth, the *Beis ha-Mikdash*, the Holy Temple in *Yerushalayim* / Jerusalem, and specifically the place of the Holy of Holies, was built on the portion of Eretz Yisrael that was allocated to the Tribe of Binyamin (לפיכך זכה בנימין הצדיק ונעשה אושפיזכן להקב"ה: *Zevachim*, 54a). Related to Kislev, the Beis haMikdash later became the scene of the Chanukah miracle where the Hidden Light was revealed, where hope and light were triumphant over sorrow and darkness.

BODY PART

Each month is connected with a specific body part. This interinclusion of the body within time empowers us to focus on and refine the spiritual properties and miraculous functionings of our physical body, as the spiral of the yearly cycle continues to turn on its Divine axis.

According to *Sefer Yetzirah*, the *Keiva* / stomach is the body part associated with Kislev. The stomach is related to sleep, the 'sense' of this month, since "food brings on sleep" (Mishnah, *Yuma*, 18a. שהמאכל מביא את השינה). Indeed, it is during sleep that the foods we ingest — literal food, as well as everything else we internalize, including the images, sounds and sensations of the day — are digested and assimilated into the body and consciousness. Sleeping and dreaming are also healing, as they sift out and purge what is toxic to us physically, emotionally and spiritually, whether food or information.

Kislev is also related to the word *Kesel* / כסל which means loins. As the Pasuk says כי־כסלי מלאו נקלה / "for my loins are full of fever" (*Tehilim*, 38:8). The loins include the lower torso and hips, the foundation upon which the upper body stands. According to the deeper teachings of the Torah, Bitachon is connected to the cosmic trait of *Netzach* / power, victory and confidence. Netzach is embodied in our right leg, which holds us up and supports our erect posture. Emunah and Bitachon are the qualities that form our spiritual-mental-emotional foundation. Kislev affords us the ability to rediscover these supporting attributes within ourselves.

ELEMENT

There are four primary elements which serve as the fundamental building blocks of creation: fire, air, water and earth. Each month is associated with one of these four elements. However, it is important to note that while manifesting physically, these elements are also meant to be understood in a much more metaphysical sense as well, as they represent numerous deeper properties, qualities, and correspondences.

Kislev is the element of fire. This may seem counterintuitive considering that Kislev is generally the darkest of months, given its proximity to the winter solstice which sometimes occurs at the end of the month or in the beginning of the following month of Teves. However, when we consider the main practice of Chanukah, which is kindling the tiny lights amidst the vast darkness of the season, as well as this month being the energy of Ohr Chozer, as we have discussed, this makes perfect sense. The fire of Kislev is the 'higher fire' mentioned earlier; the spiritual fire that burns but does not consume. It is the Hidden Light that unifies rather than separates. And it is the inner flame that we carry and kindle through the darkness of the world, which we then offer and reveal during Chanukah, that elicits the greater illumination of Hashem following the winter solstice and New Moon of Teves. During Kislev it is upon us to nurture, protect, and ignite this 'higher fire'.

TORAH PORTIONS

Over the course of each month, 4-5 weekly Torah portions are read by the community. These individual portions can be combined and viewed as a single unit based on the particular month in which they are most commonly read. Indeed, one finds, when viewing the Parshas through this calendrical lens, that an astounding array of thematic elements consistent with the spiritual energy of the month are revealed.

During Kislev we read the Torah portions of Toldos, VaYetzei, VaYishlach, VaYeshev and also sometimes Miketz. These portions are full of the subject of sleep and dreams, from Yaakov's dream of the ladder connecting Heaven and earth, to Yoseph's dreams (of the stars and the sheaves of grain bowing down to him), to the Egyptian butler's and baker's dreams (of serving Pharaoh), and finally of Pharaoh's dreams (of the skinny cows and the skinny stalks of grain swallowing the fat cows and the healthy grain). In fact, all the major dreams of the Torah occur during these portions of the Torah that are read in Kislev.

Once Moshe is introduced in the next book of the Torah, from then on HaKadosh Baruch Hu reveals Himself to Moshe through the means of waking prophecy. Dreams are different and lower than prophecy. Prophecy is *Ohr Yashar* / Direct Light, a revelation from Above to below, while prophetic dreams are more akin to *Ohr Chozer* / Reflected Light, from below to Above. The meaning of dreams are often dim and unclear, yet they can still give us a vision of a brighter future, so long as we delve deep into the mystery of the dream and ground our understanding of it in Torah wisdom. This is similar to the dynamic between Written and Oral Torah, discussed earlier; prophecy, like the Written Torah, illuminates directly, whereas dreams, like Oral Torah, require active interpretation and questioning. Prophecy is an overwhelming light, dreams are a kind of generative darkness.

Toldos is usually the first portion to be read in the month of Kislev. Toldos begins with the story of Yitzchak / Isaac, the embodiment of Gevurah, harsh *Din* / judgment or concealment, and his wife Rivkah / Rebecca who embodies a lighter form of Gevurah. For many years, their ability to have children was 'concealed' and they were barren. (The Pasuk is written visually as כי עקרה הוא / "for he is barren", whereas the pronoun is read orally as היא / "for *she* is barren." Indeed, they were both barren — מלמד ששניהם עקורים היו: *Yevamos*, 64a). Their lives are finally 'brightened' and they are blessed with children when Yitzchak is 60 years old (*Bereishis*, 25:26). 60 is the value of the letter Samach, the letter of the month. The Torah alludes to the fact that their Tefilos, prayers to have children, were similar to a pitchfork: "Just as a pitchfork overturns the grain on the threshing floor from place to place, so too, the Tefilah of the righteous overturn the mind of the Holy One, Blessed be He, from the attribute of harsh judgment to the attribute of mercy" (*Yevamos*, ibid. *Sukkah*, 14a). This is another perfect expression of Reflected Light, a light that arises from below through our *Bakasha* / requesting, emerging miraculously through layers of concealment as an arrow piercing Heaven and overturning darkness to light, judgment to mercy.

SEASON OF THE YEAR

INTRICATELY RELATED TO THE SEASONAL QUALITIES OF EACH month are the spiritual qualities of that month. When daylight lasts for either longer or shorter times, different kinds of spiritual light are being revealed on a subtle level. The physical experiences of spring are external expressions of an internal reality emanating during that time, such as the vital pulse of new life and growth. All dark and dank months reflect an energy of corresponding spiritual 'coldness', stimulating us to seek warmth. People tend to keep to themselves when winter begins and are more outgoing when summer starts. All of these psycho-physical weather patterns reflect deeper spiritual truths, as the mind-body complex is a reflection of the metaphysical qualities of the soul and spiritual realm.

"For everything there is an appointed time" (*Koheles*, 3:1). In other words, everything happens according to precise Divine timing (Rebbe Rayatz, *Sefer haMa'amarim*, Tav/Shin/Aleph, p. 59). When we left Egypt, it was the appointed time for such liberation. Indeed, Nisan is the perfect month for Exodus and Redemption. King David in *Sefer Tehilim* / The Book of Psalms says, Hashem מוציא אסירים בכושרות / "sets free the imprisoned" (*Tehilim*, 68:7). The word כושרות is related to the word כשר / *Kosher*, meaning, Hashem took us out of prison, from Egypt, in a Kosher or 'appropriate' month. Hashem took us out, says Rebbe Akiva (*Medrash Rabbah*, Bamidbar, 3:6), in a month that is perfectly suited to be taken out and to travel in the Desert, a month that is not too hot or too cold (see also Rashi, ad loc. *Mechilta d'Rebbe Yishmael*, Bo, 16, on the verse in Tehilim, 68:7. Rashi, *Sotah*, 2a).

It is thus not only that the events of the past, such as the Going Out of Egypt, occurred in the most 'historically appropriate' time for them to occur, but also at the right time of year — the season best suited for that particular expression of redemption. This is the same principle behind every *Yom Tov*: the narrative and observance of each celebration or fast reflects and refracts the light of the natural world through a spiritual lens.

Furthermore, in the months that contain a *Yom Tov* / Holy Day, that Yom Tov embodies and encapsulates the energy of the entire month in condensed form. This is true in Kislev, with regards to Chanukah. In a month that does not have a major holy day, that absence is also an expression of the unique quality of the month.

This month of Kislev is a significant time of year in the Northern Hemisphere, as it is when the days are the shortest and darkest. The month of Kislev brings us to the doorstep of the winter solstice, the longest night of the year, following which the light begins to gradually return. Depending on how the dates fall out in a particular year, this solar nadir will either occur at the end of Kislev, during Chanukah, or in the beginning of the following month of Teves. Regardless, Kislev will always contain the most potent time of darkness during the year, as it contains both the shrinking sun and the waning moon right before or during the solstice. This means that during Kislev both the sun and the moon are at their darkest points in conjunction with each other. The waning moon of the following month of Teves will always be after the winter solstice, so the days will have already begun to elongate. The darkness of Kislev is thus a 'double darkness' of both the sun and the moon.

There is a fascinating narrative retold by *Chazal* / our sages, of Adam and Chavah, after they were exiled from the garden, celebrating an eight-day Yom Tov during their first winter as the daylight began to return and lengthen following the winter solstice. This primordial celebration of light occurred during the time that would later become the eight days of Chanukah.

"When Adam — who was created in the beginning of the year, on the first day of Tishrei — noticed that during the first three months of his life the days were getting gradually shorter, he said, 'Woe is to me! Because I've sinned, the world around me is being darkened and is returning to its state of chaos and confusion: this must be the kind of death to which I have been sentenced by Heaven!' (Adam was told that if he ate from the Tree of Knowledge — which he did, he would die.) He took upon himself to pray, fast, and look within. After eight days, he noticed the Winter Solstice (literally the *Tekufas Teves*, the season of the month of Teves), and saw that indeed the days were beginning to lengthen again. 'So this is the way of the world!' he exclaimed, and he celebrated for eight days" (*Avodah Zarah*, 8a).*

Many years later, during the period of the second Beis haMikdash, in the year 139 BCE, a miracle occurred with a jug of oil and the eight day festival of Chanukah was established. The deeper level of the celebration of Chanukah, beneath the historical context, is thus primordial and seasonal — and in this way it is arguably the first Yom Tov ever celebrated by human beings.

* Adam first fasts and prays for eight straight days, as the light is decreasing and the days are getting shorter and shorter, and then celebrates for eight days as the light begins to return and the days are getting longer and longer. Interestingly enough, some years after the Chanukah story, there arose a famous debate between *Beis Shammai* / House of Shammai and *Beis Hillel* / the House of Hillel regarding how we, today, need to light the flames of a personal Menorah on Chanukah (following the destruction of the Second Beis haMikdash, as the Menorah in the Beis haMikdash was no longer being lit). Do we light eight flames on the first night, and decrease one flame each night, or do we (as is in fact the law stipulates) light one flame the first night and then increase each night until there are eight flames lit on the eighth night: *Shabbos*, 21b. Parenthetically, this argument is also dealing with the question of whether we celebrate the negation of the negative (i.e., on the first night we needed eight days of miracles in order to procure fresh pure oil, and on the second night we only needed seven days of miracles, etc.), or do we celebrate the increase of the positive (i.e., the first night represents only one day of miracles, and the second night is two days of miracles, etc.).

THE HOLY DAYS OF THE MONTH

As mentioned, "for everything there is an appointed time," and everything happens according to Divine timing: we left Egypt in the spring, the season best suited for this expression of Redemption. This is the same principle behind every *Yom Tov*, even the Rabbinic Yamim Tovim of Purim and Chanukah. In other words: The narrative and observance of Chanukah reflects and refracts the light of the natural world through a spiritual lens.

As mentioned, the winter solstice occurs either during or in very close proximity to the end of the month of Kislev. This uniquely dark point in the yearly cycle characterizes and influences many of the major themes and energies present during this month.

Throughout Kislev, the days continue to get shorter and darker as we come closer and closer to the winter solstice, the longest night of the year. In concert with this seasonal solar phenomenon, the moon too begins to wane steadily towards the end of Kislev, until its final phase during the last week of the month, when it all but completely vanishes from the sky. The confluence of these two celestial cycles produces a kind of double darkness, the low point of the sun's circuit in the sky as well as the gradual disappearance and rebirth of the moon. This overlocking pattern produces not only the longest but also the darkest nights of the year. And, even more significantly, it is precisely at that point in the calendar, when a tiny glimmer of light begins to appear in the sky again, the moon returns and daylight slowly begins to replace the darkness of night.

This mirrors the festival of Chanukah, which celebrates the historical miracle of when a small amount of oil, which would naturally burn for only a single night, was found in the desecrated Beis HaMikdash and ended up lasting for eight full nights. Eight represents a level beyond the natural cycle of seven. Seven represents creation, while eight represents redemption. The eight days thus represent a turning point, from which the darkness of the natural world morphs into the light of the world to come, when judgment and concealment shift into mercy and revelation.

Before delving more deeply into these correlations, we need to properly understand the context and history in which the Chanukah story unfolded. The story of Chanukah was not written down in a canonical text, nor does it appear in Tanach, (this is precisely the reason the Rambam chose to write the story of Chanukah in his books on Halachah), nor was it originally allowed to be 'written down' at all

(א"ר אסי למה נמשלה אסתר לשחר לומר לך מה שחר סוף כל הלילה אף אסתר סוף כל הנסים. והא איכא חנוכה? ניתנה לכתוב קא אמרינן: *Yuma*, 29a). However, it is very succinctly noted in the Gemara, so it will do us well to review and offer some context to the narrative.

THE HISTORY & TIME PERIOD OF THE CHANUKAH MIRACLE

Having built the *Beis haMikdash* / Holy Temple in *Yerushalayim* / Jerusalem, in around 833 BCE, Shelomo haMelech / King Solomon reigned supreme over the entire Land of Israel. They were idyllic times, with great material prosperity, unity among the people, and a relative peace with the neighboring states. When Shelomo passed away his kingdom dismantled and broke into two factions. There arose the Kingdom of Israel, made up of ten of the Twelve Tribes, located in the north of Israel, and the Kingdom of Yehudah / Judah, which was composed of the tribes of Yehudah and Binyamin, to the south. Yerushalayim, along with the Beis haMikdash, was located in the Kingdom of Yehudah. The citizens of the Kingdom of Yehudah were called *Yehudim*, or *Yehudi* for an individual male and *Yehudis* for an individual female. Years later, under the Roman Empire, Yehudah became known as 'Judea', and the Yehudim became known as *Judeans*, which, over time and across languages, was shortened to *Jew*.

Sometime later, in the year 555 BCE, the Assyrians, who were living to the north of Israel, conquered northern Israel and overwhelmed the Kingdom of Israel, sending the Ten Tribes into exile, dispersing them throughout their kingdom and selling them as slaves to merchants from all corners of the ancient world. As the Beis haMikdash was in the south, enfolded within the Kingdom of Yehudah, it was not tampered with nor destroyed and it remained standing for another 150 years.

When the Babylonians — to the south of Israel rose to power in the year 434 BCE, the Babylonian king, Nevuchadnetzar, marched his troops into Judah, pillaged Yerushalayim and sent many of its upper class citizens to Babylon. Nevuchadnetzar appointed a puppet king over Judah, king Tzedekia. Tzedekia was a righteous man and erroneously thought he would be able to break free from Babylon. Nevuchadnetzar was displeased, and in 425 BCE he marched again into Yerushalayim, this time laying siege to Yerushalayim and eventually destroying the Beis haMikdash on the Ninth day of the month of Av.

The Yehudim, the Jews who lived there, were then scattered into various countries in exile, although most of them were taken down to Babylon. For a period of 70 years the Babylonian exile lasted, during which time the Babylonians were defeated by the Medians and the Medians in turn by the Persians. It was during the Persian Empire, in the year 3408 (353 BCE), that permission was given by King Cyrus and later Darius for the Jews to return to Yehudah and rebuild the Beis haMikdash. Many Jews returned to their homeland, though most chose to continue living in Babylon or other countries in the Diaspora.

Civilization mimics life; what is born matures and eventually passes on. In due time the Persian Empire collapsed under the attacks of the fearless and vengeful warrior, Alexander the Great of

Macedon. Following the fall of the Persian Empire to Alexander the Great, ancient Israel, as well as most of the Near-Eastern and Mediterranean world, came under his rule. Desiring to unify his empire as a single power, he fathomed to establish a universal culture and founded the city of Alexandria in Egypt to function as the nerve center of this new empire. Then he populated the city with people from across the globe. His idea of culture was a blend of Greek mythology and philosophy with elements of Eastern modes of thinking and esotericism.

Among the Jewish people living in Yehudah (Southern Israel) there was a great number, perhaps even a majority, who adapted and embraced Greek culture; they were known as *Misyavanim* / Hellenizers. Not being satisfied with their newfound beliefs they also wished to wield power, and ultimately gained power over the other Yehudim living in Israel. As the highest Jewish position was the *Kohen Gadol* / High Priest, they attempted and at times succeeded in buying the position from the Greek authorities.

Following the death of Alexander, the Greek Empire fell apart, and was divided between his generals. Ptolemy the First took control over Egypt, to the south of Israel, while Seleucus the First began the Seleucid dynasty and took control over Syria, to the north and east of Israel. At first Israel became part of the Seleucid Empire, but later the land was conceded to Ptolemy, and so the Land of Israel fell under the control of the Greco-Egyptian Empire, known as the Ptolemaic Empire.

When Ptolemy V was too incompetent to hold onto his Empire, the Greco-Syrian Empire led by Antiochus III conquered Israel from Ptolemy. The kingdom Antiochus ruled over was known as the Seleucid Empire. Initially, Antiochus was courteous to the Jews, but over time he became disenchanted and quite cruel. When Antiochus died, his son Seleucus took over and the oppression of the Jews was further intensified.

Besides the outside forces oppressing the Jews, internally the *Misyavanim* / Hellenists' influence was increasing and they put heavy pressure on the smaller group of Torah committed Jews. The Kohen Gadol at that time was Yochanan who was deeply opposed to the influence of the Hellenists and of Greek culture, and the Hellenists in turn despised him. Once, the Emperor was notified by one of the Misyavanim of a great treasure that was being held in the Beis haMikdash. This in fact was the money collected from the half Shekels that all adult males would give annually, and was used to support the offerings. And so, Seleucus sent his minister to collect the treasure. Yochanan pleaded with him not to take the money that was allocated and donated to the Beis haMikdash, but he did not listen.

A while later the king Seleucus was killed and his brother Antiochus IV took over the reign in the year 174 BCE. Antiochus IV was a cruel man, in all respects. Although he was admirably called Epiphanes, meaning 'the gods' beloved', an esteemed historian living at the time, Polybius, gave Antiochus IV the epithet *Epimanes* / madman, which is a much more fitting title.

Needing a way to unify his Empire, Antiochus decided that he was going to implement and enforce a single faith-practice culture throughout his entire reign. This monoculture was imposed upon

Israel as well. One of the ways utilized to eradicate Jewish practice from the land was that he removed Yochanan the righteous Kohen Gadol. In his stead, he emplaced Yochanan's Hellenized brother, Yehoshua, known as Jason, and later another Hellenized leader, Menelaus.

It was a bitter time of our history, a dark time of both external oppression as well as bitter infighting. Sadly, a large number, perhaps even a majority, of Jews surrendered their beliefs and identity as Jews and chose to mimic the Greeks in dress, culture and practice.

Once, a false rumor spread that Antiochus had an accident and died, leading the practicing Jews to rebel against Menelaus who was then serving as the Kohen Gadol. When Antiochus heard the news of the internal rebellion, he instructed his legions to go kill the insurrectionist Jews. Thousands of Jews in revolt were killed as a result, *Rachmana Litzlan* / may the Compassionate One spare us. Fearing that he was losing political control of Judea, Antiochus the Wicked harshly proclaimed that anyone discovered to be teaching, studying or practicing Torah would be severely punished. The Beis haMikdash was defiled and converted to a pagan temple and he decreed all Jewish worship to be forbidden. All the Torah scrolls were confiscated and burned, and Shabbos, *Milah* / circumcision and *Chodesh* / sanctifying the new moon, were prohibited under penalty of death. (חודש / *Chodesh*, מילה / *Milah* and שבת / *Shabbos* are together numerically 1099, the same numerical value of the words בימי מתתיהו בן יוחנן / "in the times of Matisyahu the son of Yochanan". The acronym of these three Mitzvos are ח'מ'ש, Ches (*Chodesh*) Mem (*Milah*) and Shin (*Shabbos*); these three letters are the first three letters in the word חשמונאי / *Chashmona'i*.) Kosher *Shechitah*

/ slaughter was also prohibited. Many Jews were killed in those dreadfully dark times; many were martyred and murdered while defending their faith and practice of Yidishkeit.

To enforce his ambitions, Antiochus sent his men from village to village erecting idols of pagan deities in every village and forcing those who lived there to worship them. When the soldiers of Antiochus arrived in Modi'in, the village where Matisyahu the son of Yochanan the High Priest lived, they erected an altar and instructed Matisyahu to offer sacrifices to the Greek deities. Matisyahu categorically refused.

Seeing the spectacle, a Hellenized Jew decided to offer the sacrifices himself, but when he came close to the altar, Matisyahu took his sword and pierced him. A great commotion erupted, whereupon the sons of Matisyahu and their friends fell upon the officiating Syrian officers, killing many of them, while the rest fled the village.

Knowing that Antiochus would be enraged, Matisyahu and his band of youths and friends fled Modi'in and went hiding in the hills of Judea. Over time many courageous Jews joined them and they formed legions to fight their oppressors.

Under cover of night, or in other unexpected moments, they would leave their hiding places and attack enemy outposts, mainly attempting to destroy the pagan altars that were set up all over the land.

When Matisyahu's end was near, he summoned his sons and told them to continue the fight. He instructed them that in matters of counsel they should listen to their brother Shimon the Wise, and in warfare their leader should be Yehudah. Yehudah earned the sobriquet *Yehudah haMaccabee* / Yehudah the Strong or Yehudah the Hammer. It is possible that *Maccabee* refers to Yehudah's occupation as a blacksmith, thus Yehudah the Hammer. It has also been suggested that the word "hammer" referred to the shape of Yehuda's head. In those days it was the norm to give a person an alias referring to a particular body feature, such as the shape of one's head. The idea of a "hammer head" appears as well in the Mishnah regarding Kohanim (המקבן. [with the letter Kuf] *Bechoros*, 7:1); as Yehudah was a Kohen it is very well possible that during the Second Temple period giving a nickname of "hammer-head" to a Kohen was not unusual.

Acronyms are also another possible source of the term *Maccabee.* One popular deciphering is that מכבי stands for מי כמוך באילים י׳ / *Mi Kamocha baEilim Hashem* / Who is like You among the mighty, O G-d" (*Shemos*, 15:11). Alternatively (as the Chasam Sofer writes in *Toras Moshe*, Miketz), a more *Peshat* / literal interpretation is that מכבי refers to the name מתתיהו כהן בן יוחנן / Matisyahu Kohen, son of Yochanan.

Angered by the Maccabee's attacks on his troops, Antiochus sent his trusted general Apollonius to wipe out Yehudah and his followers, the Maccabees. Although the Syrian-Greek troops he sent were greater in number, more equipped and more sophisticated, nonetheless the Maccabees defeated them. Antiochus sent out another battalion and again the Maccabees defeated them. He realized that only by sending a large army and waging a full-fledged war could he defeat Yehudah and his brave fighting men, and that is what he elected to do. Yet, the Maccabees were relentless, and day after day, despite all odds, they gained the upper hand.

As small victories became bigger victories, each battle was more miraculous and extraordinary than the last, until the Maccabees were able to once again return to Yerushalayim and liberate the Temple Mount on the 24th of the month of Kislev in the year 3622 (139 BCE). While Antiochus was not fully defeated — he was still the supreme ruler of Israel, occupying the majority of the Land and even most of Yerushalayim — and it would take years of struggle before the Jews regained their own sovereignty, when the Temple mount was liberated by the Maccabees, the Jews were able to resume serving in the Beis haMikdash.

REDEDICATING THE BEIS HAMIKDASH & THE MIRACLE OIL

Entering the Beis haMikdash on the 24th of Kislev, the Maccabees first needed to clear it of idols. Yehudah and his legions then built a new *Mizbeach* / altar, as the old one was ritually contaminated. He dedicated it on the 25th of the month of Kislev in the year 3622, and they celebrated an eight-day Rededication Ceremony, with lights and festivities, as the simple translation of the word *Chanukah* suggests: חנוכת המזבח / dedication of the Mizbeach (ונראה לפרש דנקרא חנוכה ע"ש חנוכת המזבח כדאמרי' בפרק ר' ישמעאל דבית חשמונאי גנזו אבני מזבח ששקצו אנשי עו"ג לע"ז והוצרכו לבנות מזבח חדש ולכך נקרא חנוכה ולא קאמר הכא מאי חנוכה אלא מאיזה נס קבעו אותו להדליק בו נרו: Maharsha, *Shabbos,* 21b). This celebration was similar to the festivities celebrating the dedication of the *Mishkan* / Tabernacle in the Desert, which lasted for seven days whereas on the eighth day the actual proper service and initiation began (*Pesik-*

ta Rabbasi, ch. 6). It was also similar to the eight days of Sukkos, the immediately preceding Yom Tov which had not been celebrated that year in the Beis haMikdash as it was not under the domain of Klal Yisrael (thus Sukkos and Chanukah are linked: *Sefer Rokeach*, Chanukah. Thus it is understood the opinion of Beis Shammai: כנגד פרי החג. *Shabbos*, 21b).

The only other reference to 'eight' and fire in connection to the Beis haMikdash is the *Simchas Beis haShoeiva* / Rejoicing of the House of Water-drawing, a celebration during the nights of Sukkos. Our sages tell us that Rabban Shimon ben Gamlier would take eight flaming torches and toss one and catch another, juggling them, and, though all were in the air at the same time, they would not touch each other (*Sukkah*, 53a). This is a startling allusion to the eight lights of Chanukah.

Chazal / our sages, the definitive transmitters of the living tradition of the Torah, are also the ones who record and confirm our meta-history. History occurs, but what becomes relevant for future generations to remember and relive, and what becomes part of the collective 'story' of Klal Yisrael, is dependent on Chazal and the Rabbis who embody the Oral Tradition and faithfully represent the 'prophetic' collective consciousness of Klal Yisrael. The events of the Chanukah story are recorded in various texts, but the conclusive and decisive text that reveals the essential meaning of the Chanukah story, including how and why we celebrate Chanukah, is the Gemara.

In this description of Chanukah our sages begin by asking, מאי חנוכה / *Mai Chanukah* / "What is Chanukah?" Meaning: What is the miracle of Chanukah all about and why do we celebrate it by kindling flame? (*Maharsha*, ibid). Since Chanukah is not recorded in any of the books of *Tanach* / the Five Books of Moshe, the Prophets or the Later Writings, it is important to us that our sages asked this question and gave definitive reasons for the establishment of Chanukah, and why we continue to celebrate it (לפי שכל המועדים וכן ימי פורים וד' צומות מפורש בכתוב משא"כ חנוכה: Bach, *Orach Chayim*, 670:1).

Here is the Gemara text in full: "What is Chanukah? The 25th day of the month of Kislev begins the days of Chanukah, which are eight, on which lamentation for the dead and fasting are prohibited. For when the Greeks (Assyrians) entered the Beis haMikdash, they defiled all the oils therein, and when the Chashmona'im (the Maccabees) prevailed against them and defeated them, they searched and found only one cruse of oil which had the seal of the *Kohen Gadol* / High Priest, which contained oil sufficient for one day's lighting only: yet a miracle occurred and they lit the Menorah for eight days*.

* Perhaps they needed eight days in order to purify themselves and obtain new sanctified oil: seven days of purification and the eighth day to make the oil, which takes a day. Or perhaps it took eight days for new pure oil to become available. (והטעם שהוצרכו להדליק ח' ימים מאותו פך מפני שכל ישראל היו בחזקת טמאי מתים וא"א לתקן שמן טהור עד שיעברו עליהם ז' ימים מיום טומאתם ויום א' לכתישת הזיתים ותקונם להוציא מהם שמן טהור והר"ן כתב שהיה להם שמן טהור רחוק ד' ימים והוצרכו ח' ימים בין הליכה וחזרה: *Beis Yoseph*, Orach Chayim, 670). Although the actual golden Menorah was stolen by the Syrians or other looters, the Chashmona'im fashioned a Menorah from cheaper metals, like iron, and covered it with zinc: *Menachos*, 28b.

לשנה אחרת קבעום ועשאום / The following year, these days were established (to light the Menorah) and appointed as a Yom Tov to sing praise and offer thanks (*Shabbos*, 21b. קבעום קאי אהדלקה דלעיל, ועשאום קאי אהלל והודא: Bach, *Orach Chayim*, 670:2) *

---

* The first systematic work that thematically organized Halachic law and practice in a comprehensive and straightforward manner is the Rambam's *Mishneh Torah*, otherwise known as the *Yad haChazakah* or simply *The Rambam*. Generally speaking, this is a work that codifies laws and customs and is uninterested in explaining or elaborating on the source or the story behind the laws. And yet, uncharacteristically, the Rambam begins the laws of Chanukah by recounting the narrative of Chanukah. Again, unlike any other Yom Tov, the story of Chanukah is not recorded or canonized in the written parts of Torah, not even in the later writings, as is Purim. Rambam states in his introduction to the Mishneh Torah, that one only needs to read the Written Torah and his book and will thereby be able to know all of Torah (לפי שאדם קורא תורה שבכתב תחלה, ואחר כך קורא בזה, ויודע ממנו תורה שבעל פה כלה, ואינו צריך לקרות ספר אחר ביניהם). Thus, it seems the Rambam needed to write the story, otherwise the reader would not know the reasoning behind the celebration, and his book would not be complete.

Upon further examination it becomes evident that the Rambam's version of the story, at least what he finds immensely important to record, is slightly different than the account described in the Gemara. Though these differences seem insignificant to the untutored eye, further exploration reveals that these dissimilarities have major practical applications in how and why the festival is celebrated.

Our version of the Gemara speaks of the defiling of the oils and how when the Chashmona'im prevailed against their oppressors and defeated them, they searched and found only one cruse of oil with the seal of the Kohen Gadol; this contained sufficient oil for one day's lighting only, yet a miracle occurred and they lit the Menorah for eight days. The following year, these days were appointed as a Festival of "*Hallel* / praise and *Hoda'ah* / thanksgiving": *Shabbos*, 21b.

The Rambam (*Hilchos Chanukah*) writes: "In the times of the Second Temple when the Greek rulers declared harsh decrees against the Jewish people and they annulled their practice of Judaism: they did not allow them to study Torah or perform Mitzvos. And they robbed them of their money and violated their daughters. They entered the Temple, and performed all sorts of unholy acts, defiled all purities, and greatly oppressed them, until the God of our fathers had mercy on them and rescued them. And the children of the Chashmona'im, the high priests, overwhelmed them, and destroyed them, and they saved the Jews from their hand. Whereupon they established a king from the priests, and the Kingdom of Israel returned for over 200 years until the second destruction (of the Temple.) When the Jewish people were victorious over their enemies and they defeated them, it was the 25th day of Kislev. They entered the Temple and did not find pure oil there, except one jug which did not have enough to light but one day. They lit this for eight days, until they were able to crush (olives) and make new pure oil. For this reason, the sages of that generation established these eight days, which begin on the 25th of Kislev, as days of *Simchah* / joy and *Hallel* / offering praise."

Whereas the Gemara omits mentioning anything but the miracle of the found oil burning for eight nights, and that the Greeks (spiritually) defiled the pure oils, the Rambam adds an account of the physical oppression that reigned, in addition to the spiritual oppression, and speaks euphorically of the return of Jewish sovereignty in the Holy Land for a period of over 200 years — albeit in limited form. Upon closer reflection, it also seems that the Rambam does not stress the miracle of the oil, as he only writes, "and they lit it for eight days." Perhaps this is more aligned with another version in the Medrash (see also *Menachos*, 28b): "Why do we light candles on Chanukah? When the children of the high priest of Chashmona'i were victorious over the Greeks…they entered the Beis haMikdash and found eight poles of metal, affixed them and lit candles in them…." (*Pesikta Rabsi*, Parsha 2:1 Chanukah. ולמה מדליק נרות בחנוכה אלא בשעה שנצחו בניו של חשמונאי הכהן הגדול למלכות יון ...נכנסו לבית המקדש מצאו שם שמונה שפודין של ברזל וקבעו אותם והדליקו בתוכם נרות ולמה קורין את ההלל מפני שכתב ... במלכות של יון שכילה אותה הקדוש ברוך הוא התחילו נותנים הימנון ושבח). Furthermore, the Gemara says, "Days of *Hallel* / offering praise and *Hoda'ah* / thanksgiving", whereas the Rambam writes, "days of *Simchah* / joy and *Hallel* / offering praise."

These differences are not merely linguistic or semantic but are subtly suggestive, and because of them there are varying opinions as to what the miracle was exactly, and, as a result, what and how we should celebrate it. Is Chanukah primarily a spiritual celebration, and thus a time for spiritual activities such as Hallel and Hoda'ah, or is it also a celebration of the 'physical' battles that were won and the return of Jewish sovereignty, and thus a time of Simchah, meaning festive, 'physical' meals?

As, according to the Rambam, the days of Chanukah are days of Simchah, it is

In a most concise way, Chazal are telling us what Chanukah is by omission: they mostly ignore the military victory, revealing that the main purpose and relevance of these Holy Days is the miracle of the oil, the "light" and all that the oil and light represents. These points render an event that occurred thousands of years ago relevant today, and reveal how the Chanukah story is a vital part of our meta-history.

BITACHON / TRUST AND HOPE

Clearly, it was a very dark period for Klal Yisrael. There was religious persecution and people were being killed for their beliefs and practice. Matisyahu the Kohen Gadol, gathered his sons and together with a small but righteous band of warriors, fought battle after battle until they were able to re-enter the Beis haMikdash. This in itself, to go up against the mighty Syrian-Greek legions, demanded tremendous Bitachon. This group of faithful warriors, led by the family of *Kohanim* / priests certainly had great Bitachon

---

indeed a Mitzvah to eat special meals on them. However, what is the exact connection between Chanukah and Simchah? The Meshech Chochmah (*Behaalosecha*, 10:10) offers a Chidush: the Mitzvah of Simchah on Chanukah is the *Chanukas haMizbeach* / the inauguration of the newly built Mizbeach. Similarly, the Darchei Moshe (*Orach Chayim*, 670) brings down from the Ohr Zarua that the qualities of Simchah and Yom Tov were established for Chanukah because of the Chanukas haMizbeach, and Hallel and Hoda'ah were established because of the miracle with the oil: אבל במרדכי הארוך כתב ובמגילת תענית אמרו שקבעום י"ט משום חנוכת המזבח וכ"כ א"ז וכ"מ במדרש רבתי פרשת בהעלותך והכא אומר שקבעוהו משום הנס וי"ל דמשום זה קבעו משתה ושמחה אבל להלל ולהודות קבעו משום נס וכ"מ מפירש"י עכ"ל. Perhaps the Rambam understands that Chanukah demands Simcha from the fact that on Chanukah there is a Mitzvah to sing Hallel, and Hallel is recited on days of שמחה יתרה /extra joy (thus not on Rosh Hashanah and Yom Kippur. Rambam, *Hilchos Chanukah*, 3:6), thus Chanukah must be a time of Simcha.

to stand up to their oppressors and fight for their belief and freedom (כהן / *Kohen* is numerically 75, the same as the word *Bitachon*, as mentioned earlier). Despite the darkness of their time, they trusted in the Source of Life and in the possibility of miracles. This profound Bitachon in the battlefield spilled over into their lives when the Beis haMikdash was liberated. It was this movement of Bitachon that inspired them to observe a defiled, ransacked Holy Temple with a destroyed *Mizbeach* / altar and lacking a Menorah — and despite their fatigue, continue to act. They did not say, 'We won the battle, let's take the day off, or even just the night off, and come back tomorrow and see what can be salvaged. Rather, they immediately envisioned a rededication and re-purification, and acted on it.

It was their Bitachon that drove them to put together a makeshift Menorah (*Menachos*, 28b), and to believe that if they searched long and hard enough, they would find some Kosher oil to be able to rekindle the Menorah. And because they had such Bitachon, their eyes were open enough to see a small jug of pure oil. This alone was a great miracle, and yet a further miracle occurred, and the small jug of oil burned for eight nights.

Writing some 200 years after the re-dedication of the Beis haMikdash, Josephus Flavius writes that Chanukah was called the 'Festival of Lights': "From that time to this, we celebrate this festival and call it Lights. Perhaps the reason is that this liberty beyond our hopes appeared to us, and that was the name given to the festival" (*Antiquities*, VII:7. This is a book that the Poskim write contains Musar and Yiras Shamayim: *Shulchan Aruch,* Orach Chayim, 307:16, *Be'er Heitev*, *Mishnah Berurah,* ad loc. *Shulchan Aruch haRav*, ibid, 30, and can be read on Shabbos. It is recorded that Rebbetzin Rivkah (the wife of the Rebbe Maharash) would read from this text to women on Shabbos: *Reshimas haYoman,* 13). The month of Kislev empowered the Chashmona'im, and continues to empower us today, to rekindle our dreams of real, existential and spiritual freedom. When we seek it, we will find the fulfillment of our inner dreams, and tap into the possibility of the miraculous. Indeed, the *Kli* / vessel that allows all miracles to manifest is our Bitachon in HaKadosh Baruch Hu, the Infinite Source of all Life and all possibility. Let us now delve a little deeper, by first reviewing a bit about the seasonal context of Chanukah.

THE SEASONAL CONTEXT OF CHANUKAH

Generally speaking, during the summer months, people are more outgoing and extroverted and as the weather is 'lighter' they take themselves more lightly. Then, however, as the sunlight begins to dwindle, and the days begin to get colder, 'denser' and 'heavier', people tend to gravitate inward, they begin hibernating and become psychologically and often even physically, 'heavier'. After the month of Tishrei, with its relatively pleasant weather and its joyful Holy Days and celebrations, the month of Cheshvan comes along with rainy, colder weather and is completely devoid of Holy Days. During this period, people desire more often to be alone, to introspect and self-generate, as explored at length in the book, *The Month of Cheshvan: Navigating Transitions, Elevating the Fall.*

Kislev, at least the majority of the month, follows the same pattern. In Kislev, the days continue to get shorter and colder until we reach the winter solstice, the longest night of the year. At that point in the calendar, a tiny glimmer of light begins to appear and daylight slowly begins to replace the darkness of night. At the same time, a desire resurfaces in people to reconnect with others and to celebrate together. Right around this first glimmer of light and increased connectivity, Chanukah begins.

THE SPIRAL NATURE OF TIME

Chanukah was and continues to be a time for the possibility of miracles and revealing light. Chanukah will forever be celebrated, but not merely to commemorate a past event. We do not celebrate miracles of the past, per se. There is no Yom Tov, for instance, that specifically commemorates the miracle of the Manna, or the miraculous Well of Miriam in the Desert. The Yom Tov's we celebrate do 'recall' a past event, but in such a way that the Ohr and *Shefa* / flow of light is re-experienced in the present and projected into the future. Indeed, we can experience the very same Divine *Koach* / power that engendered the miracle in the first year in a higher, deeper, tangible fashion each year, as the world spirals ever closer toward the Ultimate Redemption.

After briefly describing the story of Chanukah, the sages conclude: ...לשנה אחרת / "The following year, these days were appointed as a Yom Tov to sing praise, and offer thanks" (*Shabbos*, 21b). In other words, the Yom Tov of Chanukah was only established on the first anniversary of the miracles, not the same year that the miracles happened. When the same season came around, *Chazal* / our sages realized that the same miraculous qualities that were manifest in the previous year were again available in the subsequent year, and thus they would continue to be available in all the years to come. Therefore, they established that Chanukah be celebrated every year (אך לשנה אחרת ראו חכמי הדור שאותה ההארה שהיתה בשמים למעלה בשנה שעברה שהיה בה הנס חוזרת ונתגלית בשנה זו: *Ben Yehoyada*, ad loc). Every year at the same time, the meta-source that gave rise to the original Chanukah miracles is potentially revealed again. If this were not the case, it would have been clear that they were one-time miracles, and while we may have marked this time as a historical event, it would not have real relevance to us and it would not be celebrated as a 'Yom Tov'.

What was available on Chanukah in the first year, our sages realized and intuited, is now available every year. As we recite when kindling the Menorah, "...Who created miracles for our ancestors בימים ההם בזמן הזה / in those days, at this time." Superficially this means it was during this time of year that in those days miracles occurred. Yet, more deeply this means, what occurred "in those days" is reoccurring ever since, even "at this time"; both then and now.

Chanukah is a time of miracles. During these Holy Days, when we have washed our hands for a meal with bread and are reciting *Birchas haMazon* / the Blessing after the Meal, we add the passage of על הנסים / "Upon the Miracles" during the second blessing. And what happens if one forgets to recite this passage in its appropriate location in the second blessing? According to the Rama (*Orach Chayim*, 187:4), in such a case, one should insert the phrase, הרחמן הוא יעשה לנו נסים כמו שעשה בימים ההם / "May the Merciful One create miracles for us as He has done during these days" towards the end of the Birchas haMazon and then continue with the standard על הנסים. What is puzzling about this ruling is that the general consensus of sages is that one does not pray for miracles, and yet here we are explicitly requesting miracles (*Ta'anis*, 24b. *Berachos*, 60a. Although see Yerushalmi, *Berachos* 9:3). "How can we pray for miracles?" (*Sha'arei Teshuvah*, Orach Chayim, 187:4). We do not normally ask for miracles because the way Hashem operates and interacts with the natural world is through the workings of nature, and changing nature can be seen as a negative thing (כמה גרוע אדם זה שנשתנו לו סדרי בראשית. *Shabbos*, 53b). Yet, during Chanukah time, the world is functioning from a place of miracles and thus we can rightfully dream, desire, request, and pray for miracles (*Divrei Shaul*, Derush Chanukah).

Chanukah is a time when miracles can occur, just like "in those days, at this time". This is because "for everything there is an appointed time." For example, *Yetzias Mitzrayim* / our Exodus from Egypt occurred in its historically appropriate time, and also in the most suitable time for redemption in the cycle of year: in the first month of spring, when it is not too hot or too cold. In our context, Chanukah first happened at the most appropriate time in history, and also during the most suitable time of year: late in Kislev, when the moon is waning and the sun is at its lowest point.

The story of Chanukah transpired during the Second Beis ha-Mikdash Era, precisely when Greek Hellenist culture was in full bloom. Within that period, the miracle of Chanukah needed to become outwardly manifest as a historical event. At the same time, Chanukah continues to occur as a spiritual event in the same season that Adam celebrated the re-emerging sunlight and the gradual retreat of darkness. In the month of Kislev, the month of renewed light, the miracle of Chanukah occurs as a new revelation of the *Ohr haGanuz* / the Hidden Light of Creation.

There is a cyclical nature to time, with the reoccurring seasons of the year, and there is the linear dimension of time, in which time and history are constantly progressing forward. Every year we circle through the very same points in the calendar: spring, summer, fall and winter, and yet time is also moving forward.

A spiral is simultaneously cyclical and linear — this is indeed the nature of time. Although every year we journey around the same cycle and the coordinates and landscape of seasons and Holy Days, every year we are spiraling into a deeper vantage point, a higher evolution of consciousness. 'Time' is not merely linear, like points of time strung together in a chain of fixed causality. As we relive and re-experience these spiritual 'pressure points' along the yearly cycle, we are given the chance to rise above past limitations and create more illumination than before, in relation to those very same moments, experiences, and complexes of meaning .

Life and events are not merely happening to us, but within us. Knowing this gives us the choice and ability to elevate ourselves with every passing year, every birthday, every Rosh Hashanah, every Yom Kippur, every Chanukah, and every day.

Each year when Chanukah arrives, not only can we tap into the Divine *Koach* / power and *Shefa* / flow that gave rise to the miracle of Chanukah in the first year, we can also tap into a higher, more essential version of it. Because of the cyclical dynamic of time, the Divine qualities of Kislev today are the same as they were originally. This enables us to tap into those qualities in the present era. Yet, since time is also progressing forward, in many ways what is available today is even deeper than what was available in the past. Every year a higher and deeper Light of Hashem is revealed in the world

(ובכל שנה ושנה יורד ומאיר מחכמה עילאה אור חדש ומחודש שלא היה מאיר עדיין מעולם: *Tanya*, Igeres HaKodesh, 14). Thus, beyond re-experiencing the power of the original miracle, we can reveal an even greater manifestation of that ever-evolving power.

TRUSTING THE LIGHT

As we have observed regarding the original Chanukah miracle, it was their Bitachon that created the context and opened the possibility for such a miracle to occur. The same is true for us as well. Bitachon in HaKadosh Baruch Hu and in Hashem's goodness is the *Kli* / vessel that allows for miracles to occur. As explored earlier, the etymological root of the word *Kislev* means 'trust' and 'hope'.

At first, as daylight is getting shorter and shorter, a feeling of depression may set in. A lack of sunlight can lead to Seasonal Affective Disorder, or at least a feeling of melancholy. Everything looks gloomy. Yet just when this season has attained its crescendo with waning moon of Kislev and the winter solstice, a small but drastic turn occurs and daylight begins to lengthen again. This glimmer of warm light, appearing at the end of a cold darkness, is sufficient enough to relieve a person of their winter depression and give them hope in a brighter future. Psychologically, this natural phenomenon stimulates or confirms our sense of Bitachon.

THE DARKEST MOMENT

Historically, the context of the narrative of Chanukah occurred in a dark time in our history (וחושך זו גלות יון / "And darkness, this refers to the Greek Exile": *Medrash Rabbah*, Bereishis, 2:4). The story occurred in the darkest possible time of year. Not only does the period of Chanukah fall within close proximity to (sometimes even containing) the winter solstice, which makes it the longest night of the solar year, it also contains the darkest nights according to the lunar calendar. When collating the solar and lunar calendars, the longest night of the year is not necessarily the darkest. If, for example, the longest night of the year would fall out at the midpoint of the lunar cycle — on the 15th of the month — the night might be the longest, but there will be a bright full moon. However, the period with the least moonlight occurs during the last week of each monthly cycle — the night of concealment before the revelation of the thin sliver of the new moon. Therefore, since Chanukah occurs in the last week of Kislev, the nights of Chanukah are the darkest of the year in terms of having the least sunlight as well as the least moonlight.

Rav Yaakov Yosef, a student of the Baal Shem Tov, calculates that the night the Chashmona'im were victorious — the night they searched and found a small jug of oil and lit the Menorah — was precisely, that year, the longest night of the year. This is the ultimate Bitachon in the face of all odds, despite what the 'world' was telling them, the Chashmona'im fought valiantly and trusted in Hashem and in themselves that they could be victorious, and they were. They trusted that they would find some oil, and they did. And their trust became the vessel in which the Chanukah miracle occurred.

By Divine orchestration, that first evening of the dedication and the kindling of the Menorah, the 25th of Kislev, is the exact same date that Antiochus had a pagan altar erected in the Beis haMikdash, three years prior. Indeed, a dark day was turned into a day of light and thanks-giving.

THE DEEPER MIRACLE

It took incredible Bitachon for the Chashmona'im to stand up to the Greek oppressors, and this Bitachon is what led them to victory. But an even greater measure of Bitachon was manifest 'after' the battle for Yerushalayim and the Beis haMikdash. It is one thing to have Bitachon while the adrenaline of war is in full throttle. It is entirely another thing to continue to have the same Bitachon once arms are laid down.

When the Chashmona'im were finally able to re-enter the Holy Beis haMikdash, instead of collapsing from exhaustion they were determined to immediately rekindle the Menorah and begin the rededication.

Many people, upon entering the Temple Mount would have observed the Beis haMikdash and decided to first clean up the mess, to take a few days to recuperate, and then begin to rededicate it. Many people would have interpreted the mess as too overwhelming and would have nominated a cleaning committee to deal with it. Yet, the Chashmona'im did the exact opposite; despite the fact that everything holy seemed to have been violated and rendered impure and that the Beis haMikdash lay in shambles and the Land of Israel in chaos, they entered into the Beis haMikdash and the first thing they did was start looking for pure oil.

Given the fact that the Beis haMikdash had been systematically desecrated and was a chaotic mess, it would have been understandable had they rejected even the thought of stopping then and there to look for pure oil to kindle the Menorah. The Menorah had in fact been stolen and no pure oil was to be seen or expected. Herein lies the greatest miracle: their resolute Bitachon itself. The real miracle was their steadfast, logic-defying Bitachon that a) they had the strength, on the very night the battle ended, to look for the oil, and that b) if they looked hard enough they would find what they were looking for. In truth it is only because they looked for it that they found the pure oil, and that the miracle of the light occurred.

Their Bitachon to look and to find was itself the *Keli* / vessel that engendered and allowed the miracle of one night's worth of oil to last for eight full nights — the time that they needed in order to rededicate the Beis haMikdash and create a new batch of fresh pure oil. Through their miraculous Bitachon they were able to light up the deepest darkness, reveal their hidden, innermost light and thus allow for the Ohr haGanuz to shine brightly on the Menorah.

We need to create the vessels for miracles to occur. Without the vessel of spiritual desire, the desire to rekindle the Menorah, no miracle would have happened. Furthermore, in the stark language of the Zohar, not only would the miracle of Chanukah not have occurred, but we would have been lost as a people: "If not for HaKadosh Baruch Hu awakening the desire in the hearts of the Cohanim, the Chashmona'im, to kindle the Menorah with olive oil, the Jewish People would have vanished from this world" (לולי שהעיר הקדוש ברוך הוא רוח הכהנים, שהיו מדליקין נרות בשמן זית, אזי אבדה פליטת יהודה מן העולם: *Zohar Chadash,* Noach 142). The courage, stamina, determination, belief and trust to look for oil, despite the fact that it seemed like an exercise in futility — and to light it, despite the fact that they only had enough to last for one night, demonstrates the *Netzach Yisrael* / the unwavering Bitachon of Klal Yisrael, and the meta-root of our very existence.

Klal Yisrael is a people that lives on and flourishes despite all odds. Despite the tremendous hardships of exiles and persecutions, pogroms and massacres, we have always risen from the ashes and forged on. We are "believers, the sons of believers". We live in this world, and yet our aspirations, visions, hopes and longings, are for the future, for the World to Come, the world of redemption, perfection, and peace.

Not only do we believe in the seemingly impossible, in the miraculous, we *are* a miracle. Our very existence is the greatest miracle of all history.

The first known record and the first time the Jewish people are mentioned in any context outside the Torah, is the "Merneptah Stele" found in Thebes, dated the year 1007 BCE. Scripted in hieroglyphics, the following is written: "Canaan has been plundered into every sort of woe, Ashkelon has been overcome, Gezer has been captured, Yanoam has made nonexistent, Israel is laid waste, his seed is no more." Simply put, the very first reference in any text, code or stele is that the People of Israel had been destroyed, without any living descendants. And yet, here we stand, thousands of years later, long after the collapse of the Egyptian, Babylonian, Persian, Greek and Roman civilizations. Against all logic we are flourishing, growing, dreaming and aspiring, desiring only to bring more and more light into the world.

The courage to look for sanctified oil, the Bitachon to kindle just one small jug of oil, is part of who we are, believers and descendants of believers. Because of this, we are a living, breathing, ongoing wonder of wonders.

When the Chashmona'im miraculously searched for, found and lit the small jug of oil, the oil of Bitachon, it unleashed the most powerful light of the universe, the Ohr haGanuz, the primordial 'Hidden Light', within themselves and throughout Creation. This awesome, otherworldly light has no relation to any amount of oil; it has no need to burn or consume any substance in order to shine. It does not need to eliminate another to exist. This is why the lights of the Menorah remained lit for eight nights, long after any single jug could physically allow, as will now be explained.

WHY IS CHANUKAH EIGHT NIGHTS?

Chazal / our sages tell us that "they found only one jug of oil which lay with the seal of the High Priest, which contained sufficient oil for one day's lighting only (ולא היה בו אלא להדליק יום אחד): yet a miracle occurred and they lit (the Menorah) with that oil for eight days." If this is the case we should celebrate Chanukah for seven days, as there was sufficient oil for one day, and the miracle started only after the first day, lasting for seven days. Why is Chanukah then celebrated for eight days if the miracle was only for seven? This is one of the most discussed questions of the sages regarding Chanukah (*Beis Yoseph*, Orach Chayim, 670), and various answers are offered.

Perhaps the simplest answer is that while the miraculous event with the oil indeed occurred on only seven nights, the first day of Chanukah celebrates the military victory, the miraculous triumph over oppression and persecution — and the manner in which Holy

Days are celebrated is with lights and festivities. Yet, this answer does not fit with the emphasis of Chazal on the miracle of the oil, and their deemphasis of the military victory (although, this does fit with other Medrashim and the Rambam's version of the events).

In one early version of the recorded teachings of Chazal, the *Sheiltos d'Rav Achai Ga'on* (26:4), it is written that the jug of oil did not have adequate oil 'even for one day', and as such, the fact that it lit for any substantial amount of time, even one day, was a miraculous occurrence. In this way, it was an eight day miracle. The more known version, however, is that they found a jug of oil that *was* sufficient for one night and it lasted eight nights. If so, there were only seven miraculous nights; why then do we celebrate eight nights?

There are other reasons offered — besides the miracle of oil — as to why Chanukah is an eight day festival. For example, when the *Mishkan* / Tabernacle was originally dedicated in the Desert, they initiated the process with seven days and then on the eighth day they actually dedicated it and began the service. Thus, the Chashmona'im too wished to rededicate the Beis haMikdash with an eight day celebration (as alluded to in the *Pesikta Rabbasi*, 6. את מוצא זאת החנוכה שאנו עושים זכר לחנוכת בית חשמונאי על שעשו מלחמה ונצחו לבני יוון ואנו עכשיו מדליקין וכן בשעה שנגמרה מלאכת המשכן עשו חנוכה*). *Megilas Ta'anis* (Ch. 9) writes that the rededication lasted eight days because it took the Chashmona'im

---

* Indeed, they began to build the Mishkan itself on the 15th of Tishrei, the first day of Sukkos (marking the return of the Clouds of Glory: see *Pirush haGra*, Shir haShirim, in the beginning, and *Pirush haGra*, Mishlei, 30:4). The construction was concluded on the 25th day of Kislev, which would, centuries later, become the first day of Chanukah. As the Tur writes, ומפרש בפסיקתא משום שנשלם מלאכת המשכן בכ"ה כסליו / "As explicitly written in the Pesikta: '...as the construction of the Mishkan concluded on the 25th day of Kislev'": *Tur*, Orach Chayim, 684.

eight days to rebuild the altar and repair the damage of the ransacked Beis haMikdash (see also *Ohr Zarua* on Hilchos Chanukah).

Also, perhaps Chanukah is an eight day celebration because the *Bris Milah* / circumcision is performed on the eighth day of a boy's life. Since the Greeks wanted to eradicate the Mitzvah of Milah, we celebrate our spiritual victory over them for eight days (כבר בארנו ח׳ ימים למה. ויש נותנים טעם אחר לדבר לפי שבטלו להם מצות מילה שהיא לשמונה לפיכך קבעו ח׳ ימי חנוכה כך כתב הבעל העתים ז״ל: *Kol Bo*, Siman 44:24).

Yet, in the Gemara, Chazal tell us that the eight day celebration of Chanukah is intricately connected with the miracle of the oil. So the question remains: why eight days and not seven, as most accounts based on the oil imply that the miracle lasted only seven days?

The Chasam Sofer answers that when the Chashmona'im saw the Beis haMikdash defiled in shambles, they decided to take the Menorah outside, to the courtyard and kindle the Menorah there with the small jug of oil (Which according to the Rambam is allowed to be done. לפיכך אם הטיב הכהן את הנרות והוציאן לחוץ מתר לזר להדליקן. Hilchos *Bi'as HaMikdash*, 9:7, although the Ra'avad writes, הפליג כשאמר מותר לזר להדליקן אלא שאם הדליקן כשירות). In normal circumstances, when the Menorah was burning inside the Beis haMikdash, one small jug of oil would have lasted the whole night. But outside, with the wind blowing, more oil was required, and yet the flames lasted throughout the night — this was the miracle of the oil on the first night (*Derashos Chasam* Sofer, Chanukah, p, 67). This courageous act of the Chashmona'im, to reveal and advertise the light for all to see, is perhaps the root of our practice to place the Chanukah lights in public view, by our doors or windows.

Rav Yoseph Caro, the *Mechaber* / celebrated author of the *Shulchan Aruch* / The Code of Jewish Law, in an earlier commentary called Beis Yoseph, deals with this question and offers three alternative solutions:

A) Originally, when they found the jug of oil that technically could only have lasted one day, they knew that they needed to light the Menorah every night for the next eight nights until they could produce fresh pure oil. They devised a plan and poured the oil into eight smaller containers. Each night they poured one of these smaller containers into the lamps of the Menorah, and on each subsequent night a miracle occurred: a minuscule measurement of oil fueled the Menorah the entire night. As such, on every night a new miracle transpired (see also Meiri, *Shabbos*, 21b).

B) After emptying out the entire jug of oil into the lamps of the Menorah on the first night, they found that the jug mysteriously remained full of oil. Each night, they emptied all the oil from the jug, and yet each night the jug remained full, as if replenished on its own. This miracle reoccurred on all eight nights.

C) On the first night they poured all the oil into the lamps of the Menorah and the next day they found that miraculous new oil had refilled the Menorah. This miracle occurred on each of the eight days.

Later commentators questioned these explanations and offered their own interpretations. The trouble with the first answer in *Beis Yoseph* regarding pouring the oil into eight containers, is that there is a principle (certainly with regard to the Beis haMikdash) that לא סמכינן אניסא / "One should not rely on a miracle" (*Pesachim*, 64b. See also

Rosh, on Tamid, 31b. *Machzor Vitri*, Avos, 5:5. (ואעפ"י שלא אירע קרי. לא סמכינן אניסא). How could they divide the oil into eight, relying on a supernatural event that each of the smaller measurements would last the entire night? If they would not have divided the oil into eight portions, at least they would have been able to light the Menorah properly for one full night.

Besides, as many ask (Maharal, *Ner Mitzvah*, p 21. *Pri Chadosh*, Orach Chayim, 670), another principle of the Beis haMikdash service is that one ought to fill all the vessels in the Beis haMikdash to the brim. In the case of the Menorah the proper way of filling it with oil is to fill it completely. The Torah tells us that the Menorah needed to "burn from evening to morning" (*Vayikra*, 24:3). According to our sages, this teaches us to "provide it with a requisite measure so that it (the Menorah) may burn from evening until morning" (מערב עד בקר תן לה: מדתה שתהא דולקת והולכת מערב עד בקר *Menachos*, 89a). This clearly suggests that the proper way would have been to empty the entire jug of oil into the lamps of the Menorah on the first night. The scholarly Chashmona'im would have been well aware of this.

According to the last two answers, the oil itself was miraculous; whether it was new miracle oil in the jug or new miracle oil found in the Menorah. Yet such 'miracle' oil would not be actual olive oil (*Klei Chemdah*, Vayakhel, 35:27-28). The Torah's definition of oil is 'natural': a liquid that is squeezed from olives, not a substance that comes 'from Heaven'. Miracle oil, however it is understood, might burn and create light, but it is not technically the 'olive oil' that is required for the Menorah service (see Radak, *Melachim 2*, 4 regarding the miraculous oil and its exemption from tithing. *Menachos*, 69b, *Tosefos* ad loc). This is a question recorded in the name of Rav Chayim Brisker.*

* See the Stiepler, *Sha'arei Tevunah*, Siman 5. This seems also to be the opin-

Above are the three known reasons given by the Beis Yoseph and their difficulties. Below are additional answers.

D) The Taz comments that none of the above answers of the Beis Yoseph are written clearly in the Gemara, but our sages should have documented what was done with the oil, whether it was divided into eight containers or whether miraculous oil appeared, so that we could know exactly what we are celebrating. Miracles and blessings need a physical vessel in order to take hold; as the Zohar explains, spirituality requires a resting place in physicality in order to be revealed. Therefore, writes the Taz, the miraculous potency of the oil needed a small amount of actual, physical olive oil to have

---

ion of the Rebbe, the Tzemach Tzedek: *Reshimos*, vol. 174. Although, as the Rebbe writes, it is possible that when the Torah says we need to use "olive oil", it merely means that it needs to have the *qualities* of olive oil, such as משך נהורי טפי / it burns with a clearer light: *Shabbos*, 23a, or, נמשך אחר הפתילה טפי מכולה / "it draws itself to the wick more than all other oils": Tosefos, *Shabbos*, ibid. Also, actual olive oil should be used because it is connected to *Chochmah* / wisdom (*Menachos*, 85b. *Berachos*, 57a, regarding seeing olive oil in a dream), and the Menorah is connected with Chochmah, הרוצה שיחכים ידרים: *Baba Basra*, 25b.

Rav Baruch Ber answers this question as follows. Clearly, besides the main ritual Menorah, the Beis haMikdash had many other Menorahs throughout, for the purpose of illumination. And so Rav Baruch Ber suggests, that upon entering the Beis haMikdash on the 25th of Kislev, and finding it and the Mizbeach in ruins, they did not, nor were they allowed, to kindle the actual Menorah, as the Menorah cannot be lit without a properly functioning Mizbeach (*Yerushalmi*, *Shekalim* 4). The procedure of dedicating the Mizbeach is eight days, thus, on the eight day of Chanukah we read in the Torah, "This is the dedication of the Mizbeach." What they did kindle was a Menorah to generate light, and miraculously the oil lasted for eight nights. Being that we are not dealing with the ritual Menorah, they indeed could have poured the oil into eight smaller containers, and they could have filled the Menorah with a small amount of oil, and they could have used any oil, even Heavenly, miraculous oil.

a *Cholas* / holding and to reveal the miracle of eight days of light. Following the first night, when a small measure of oil remained lit throughout the night, an even smaller amount of that oil remained in the Menorah as a Cholas for the second night. This shows that the first night was also a miracle, as after burning, some of that original physical olive oil remained in the lamps throughout each of the next seven nights, allowing the Divine miracle to rest upon it. (The Tzemach Tzedek has a variation of this interpretation, and he once reportedly remarked that if *no* oil remained after the first night, then the oil of the next seven days would have been 'miracle oil' and not olive oil, and olive oil is needed for the Menorah: *Reshimos*, Vol. 174.)

E) It could be argued that the first day of Chanukah celebrates the miraculous *finding* of the jug of oil, although it would have been a miracle "vested within the workings of nature". The fact that they found a cruse of pure oil, uncharacteristically sealed with the seal of the high priest, is nothing less than miraculous (*Chasam Sofer*, Derashos). In this scenario, the first day is celebrated for the finding of the oil, and the next seven days are celebrated for the miracle of the oil continuing to burn.

On a deeper level, perhaps the miraculous burning of the oil for seven nights retroactively revealed to our sages the miraculous nature of the finding of the oil. The first day we celebrate the actual finding of the jug, and the following seven days demonstrate to us that even natural events, such as finding pure oil in a systematically desecrated Temple, are in themselves miraculous.

F) Even deeper, we can suggest that the first day is not so much a celebration of the miraculous oil, but rather for the miraculous people; not for the *Cheftzah* / object, but rather for the *Gavrah* /

person. The first night and day of Chanukah we celebrate the will, stamina and tenacity of the Chashmona'im, who, having found the Beis haMikdash in shambles, did not surrender to the circumstances and say, 'Let's wait eight days until we produce new oil, or at least until the morning, to search the area for any remains.' Instead, they had the audacity to search then and there, in the darkness of the night and the desecrated Temple. They had the audacity to believe that if they would search hard and long enough they would find pure oil, and that is exactly what happened, they found the oil: and not only was it enough to burn for that one night, but for another seven miraculous nights as well. We too, in the depths of the winter, light up our Menorahs when night descends, knowing that if we search hard and long enough we too will find the fuel we need to triumph over all darkness and bring light to the world.

On Chanukah we are celebrating the stamina, Emunah and Bitachon of the Chashmona'im, the fact that they 'miraculously' looked for pure oil amidst the ruins and did not give up even when the 'chances' of finding even a single drop seemed illogical or impossible. And we are celebrating ourselves, that despite the darkness of the world, we too are looking faithfully for a 'small jug of oil' that will light up the long night of exile, that will light up the world.

FIRE VS. LIGHT

Let us go back to the simple reading of the Gemara: "They found only one jug of oil with the seal of the High Priest, containing sufficient oil for only one day's lighting. Yet a miracle occurred and they lit (the Menorah) with that oil for eight days." The question we have been digging into more and more deeply is, why do we consider all eight nights to be nights of miracles, and not just seven nights? It would seem, if basing one's counting on the oil itself, that the first night was not a miracle as there was enough oil for the first night. We will now delve into an innovative mystical answer.

G) Normally, for fire to exist it needs to consume oil, wick, or any other object. To produce light it must destroy; its 'life' is dependent on the consumption or annihilation of another entity. Yet, there is a higher form of *Ohr* / light, a Heavenly Light that brings warmth and illumination without the need to consume anything. It was this light that became revealed on Chanukah. For eight nights of Chanukah, a mysterious, higher fire burned brightly on the Menorah, without devouring a wick or consuming oil. In other words the miracle was in the *Ohr* / the actual light or fire itself, and not in the oil, the *Kli* / vessel. The miracle was not in a small amount of oil burning for eight days, nor a miraculous new oil appearing in the jug or in the Menorah — the miracle was in the light, the fire itself (the Rebbe, *Likutei Sichos*, 15). This miraculous higher light and fire is what burned on all eight long nights. It was the *Ohr haGanuz* / the Hidden Light of Creation, the 36 lights of Gan Eden, and this is the Ohr that continues to be revealed on all eight days of Chanukah, in every era.

TWO LIGHTS WITHIN ONE FLAME

Speaking about a flame of fire the *Zohar* teaches as follows: "Within the flame itself there are two lights: one is white and luminous, and the other black or blue. The white light is the higher of the two and it rises steadily. The black or blue light is underneath the white light which rests on the black or blue light as on a pedestal. The two lights are inseparably connected. The white resting upon and enthroned upon the black…The blue or black base is, in turn, attached to something beneath it (the wick), which keeps it aflame and impels it to cling to the white light above. This blue or black light sometimes turns red, but the white light above it never changes color…The lower light always consumes anything under it, or anything brought in contact with it, for such is its nature; to be a source of destruction and decay. But the white light which is above it, never consumes or destroys and never changes" (תא חזי, בשלהובא דסלקא אית תרין נהורין. חד נהורא חוורא דנהיר וחד נהורא דאתאחיד בה אוכמא או תכלא. ההוא נהורא חוורא איהו לעילא וסלקא באורח מישור. ותחותיה ההוא נהורא תכלא או אוכמא דאיהו כרסיא לההוא חוורא...ודא תכלא אוכמא לזמנין אתהדר סומקא. וההוא נהורא חוורא דעליה לא אשתני לעלמין דהא חוורא הוא תדיר. אבל האי תכלא אשתני לגוונין אלין. לזמנין תכלא או אוכמא. ולזמנין סומקא....ודא אכלא תדיר ושצי לההוא מלה דשויין ליה. דהא בכל מה דאתדבק ביה לתתא ושריא עלוי ההוא נהורא תכלא שצי ליה ואכיל ליה. בגין דאורחוי הוא לשיצאה ולמהוי אכיל. דהא ביה תליא שצו דכלא מותא דכלא. ובגיני כך איהי אכיל כל מה דאתדבק ביה לתתא. וההוא נהורא חוורא דשריא עלוי לא אכיל ולא שצי לעלמין ולא אשתני נהוריה: *Zohar* I, 51a).

To simplify, there are two main differences between the lower light and the higher light: a) the lower light continually fluctuates and changes colors, whereas the higher light is constant: b) the lower fire needs to consume and destroy another in order to exist, while the higher light does not.

Within the flame, the lower fire which is denser and darker, fluctuating between shades of red and blue, represents the natural, ever unfolding, evolving and changing physical world. In this realm of existence, life feeds off death. Organisms live by consuming and destroying other organisms. In this way, among others, everything is continually fluctuating and changing in appearance and form.

After a living body has served its purpose, it gradually rejoins the earth and becomes the soil upon which new life grows. Mineral becomes plant, plant becomes animal, animal becomes human, and human eventually returns to the minerals of the earth. In order for physical fire to exist, it must destroy its fuel, as all physical organisms must kill other organisms in order to live. This is the lower element within the flame. The higher, white, more transparent fire represents the soul, the inner light, which does not need to overwhelm or negate an 'other' in order to exist. It exists without consuming, swallowing or killing another. Deeper levels of soul are represented by more transparent shades of white light.* Near the peak of the flame it becomes so transparent that the fire is almost invisible, merging into the infinity of space. This is the unchanging, uninfluenced *essence* of the self that observes or registers the forever changing self, 'below'.

---

* Whereas the Zohar mentions only two lights in a flame, בשלהובא דסלקא אית תרין נהורין, a deeper reading of the Zohar reveals that there are three colors or shades of light in a flame: white, blue/black, and red (See Rashi, *Berachos*, 52b: שלהבת אדומה לבנה וירקרקת). The Gra (on the beginning of *Yechezkel*) speaks of three lights. נוגה / *Nogah* / 'glow' is the glow around the fire. אש / *Aish* / 'fire' is the changing color fire. And חשמל / *Chashmal*, the fire or white empty place right near the wick (very transparent light: see *Metzudas David*, Yechezkel, 1:27. With regards to the light near the wick, see also the Shaloh haKodesh, where he associates this light with the Sefirah of Malchus. *Siddur Shaloh,* Sha'ar haShamayim, Kabbalas Shabbos, Bameh Madlikin). Thus in addition to the white, blue/black and red fires, there is also an Ohr Chashmal, an 'empty' fire near the wick. Thus there are four shades or colors: the glow above, the red fire, underneath the blue/black fire, and the empty fire below. Counting the entirety of the flame itself, there are five dimensions. We could therefore suggest that the upper fire, the white glow, is associated with the Name of Hashem, Havayah. The red fire is associated with *Elokim* / judgment. The ever-changing fire, the blue/black fire, is associated with the Name Ehe'yeh. The Chashmal, the white empty fire, the base of the flame, is associated with the Name Ado-noi. The entirety of the flame itself is beyond all Names and inclusive of all Names.

Ohr haGanuz is reflected in the higher fire of the flame: it flows freely, clearly, without ever changing colors, and does not (overtly) consume the wick or oil to exist, it is entirely independent and self-sufficient.

MOSHE & THE BURNING BUSH

Moshe encountered this primordial light at the Burning Bush. The future leader of Klal Yisrael, the receiver of the Torah, sees a bush burning without being consumed, and says to himself, אסרה־נא ואראה את־המראה הגדל הזה מדוע לא־יבער הסנה / "I must turn aside to look at this marvelous sight; why does not the bush burn up (*Shemos*, 3:3)?" He is dumbfounded by this phenomenon. What Moshe witnesses and beholds that day, the day he becomes chosen to lead Klal Yisrael out of Egypt, is the Light of Gan Eden, the Ohr haGanuz. This is the higher, Divine Light that illuminates and burns, but does not destroy. This is the primordial, original Light of Creation, the Light of Day One, when Hashem said "Let there be *Ohr* / Light, and there *was* Light."

In the Creation story, on Day One, the word *Ohr* appears five times (see, *Zohar 2*, p. 167a). Interestingly, the word סנה / *S'neh* / bush appears five times in the story of Moshe, as he is encountering the Ohr. Perhaps this is the Torah's way of hinting that Moshe, in the beginning of the Book of Shemos, experienced the Light that was created on the First Day of Creation as described in the beginning of the Book of Bereishis.

This fire that Moshe encountered at the Burning Bush, at the beginning of our collective redemption from the physical, mental, emotional and spiritual oppression in Egypt, is the same fire that descended upon the Menorah for eight nights. There was luminescence, yet neither the bush nor the oil were burnt. The Chashmona'im kindled flames with natural oil, as the law mandates, and Hashem 'kindled' a natural bush. Yet the fire that rested upon them both was mysterious, miraculous: the fire of the Ohr haGanuz.

The Ohr of the First Day of Creation, which was the 25th of Elul (or Adar) became revealed many years later on the 25th of Kislev, in the story of Chanukah. *Chanukah* is spelled חנוכה, which, when divided, spells the words חנו כ"ה / 'rested on the 25th day', as the Chashmona'im rested from battle on the 25th of Kislev (Ran on *Shabbos*, 21b: It should be really called נחו כ"ה not חנו כ"ה, but if it was called נחו כ"ה one would think that mundane work would not be allowed to be done on this Yom Tov, thus Chazal called it *Chanukah*). חנו כ"ה also alludes to the resting of the Ohr haGanuz on the 25th, as it rested upon the bush and the Menorah. Appropriately, the 25th word in the Torah is *Ohr*.

From the 25th of Elul to the 25th of Kislev is three months. The process of gestation and birth is nine months, but at the three-month mark, הוכר העובר / "the fetus becomes known" (*Niddah*, 8b. וכמה הכרת העובר סומכוס אומר משום רבי מאיר שלשה חדשים: Shulchan Aruch, Yoreh De'ah, 189:33). The creation and first manifestation of the Ohr haGanuz was expressed with the declaration *Yehi Ohr* / "Let there be Light", on the 25th of Elul, but the 'fetus' only became known on the 25th of Kislev (*Sheim miShemuel*, Chanukah, 221). Creation began on the 25th of Elul but it could be said that it was not fully 'completed' until the 25th of Kislev millennia later, with the completion of the building of the Mishkan (Pesikta, *Tur*, Orach Chayim, 684). In other words, the Mishkan was a microcosm of all of Creation (*Tanchumah*, Pekudei 2), including both the physical as well as the spiritual realms (Ramban, Shemos, 31:2), and its construction paralleled the Creator's act of creation (*Zohar* 2, 152a). Yet, the true state of הוכר העובר, the recognition of the 'fetus' of Creation, was not until the revealing of the Ohr haGanuz in the miracle of Chanukah.

ON THE 25TH DAY OF KISLEV

On every 25th of Kislev since the year of the Chanukah miracle, there is a revealing of the same Ohr that was revealed to Moshe at the Burning Bush and on the First Day of Creation. Fascinatingly, many years prior to the Chanukah story, during the year of the Exodus from Egypt, on the 25th of Kislev, there was another revelation of this higher Light. The eighth plague in Egypt was the Plague of Darkness. Regarding this plague it says, "People could not see one another, and for three days no one could get up from where he was: however, all the children of Israel, enjoyed אור / light in their dwellings" (*Shemos*, 10:23). This Ohr that Klal Yisrael experienced in the depth of the darkness of Egypt was the Ohr of the First Day of Creation and the Ohr reserved for the end of time. The dwellings of Klal Yisrael were filled with the Ohr haGanuz, as Chazal tell us (*Medrash Tehilim*, Chap, 27:1).

Each of the Ten Plagues lasted one month, according to many opinions (*Medrash Rabbah*, Shemos 9). The first few weeks of each month was a period of warning that a plague was about to ensue, and in the final week the actual plague began. The Ten Plagues began in Nisan — the year prior to the Exodus, and so the Ninth Plague was in the ninth month of that year, Kislev. The actual

Plague of Darkness began in the last week of the month, meaning the 24th of Kislev, during the day, when otherwise there would have been natural light (*Shach*, ibid). Because Klal Yisrael would have enjoyed light during the day had there been no *Makah* / Plague or miracle, the beginning of the Makah was not as dramatically perceptible for them. But when the natural darkness of night descended on the evening of the 25th of Kislev, this is when Klal Yisrael fully appreciated the miracle of אור / light in their dwellings; when they were clearly experiencing the Ohr haGanuz — the Light of Creation, the Light of the Burning Bush, the Light of Chanukah.

Through their Bitachon and determination the Chashmona'im created a vessel to reveal this very same Light on the 25th night of Kislev, and for the next seven nights the Ohr haGanuz, the higher "white fire" that brings illumination, warmth and clarity, without consuming or destroying anything in the process. Along with the physical oil, their persistent action, faith and trust, were *Keilim* / vessels that allowed for the revelation of the higher, hidden Light within Creation. They had tapped into a state similar to Moshe's at the Burning Bush, Klal Yisrael's in the Plague of Darkness, and Adam and Chavah's during their 36 hours in Gan Eden. We too, standing on their shoulders, have the opportunity to tap into this state and behold this Light as we kindle the 36 lamps of Chanukah.

Nothing is a mere coincidence, certainly not cosmic events that impact all of history and Klal Yisrael. Not randomly, the miracle of Chanukah occurred 207 years before the destruction of the Second Beis haMikdash. The number 207 in letters is Reish/200 and Zayin/7. These two words spell out the word רז / *Raz* / secret, that which is hidden. It is also the numerical value of the word אור / *Ohr*

/ Light. These correspondences affirm the fact that 207 years before the destruction of the Second Beis haMikdash, the secret, hidden Light was revealed. Through their great Bitachon the Chashmona'im created the vessels that allowed for the revelation of the Ohr haGanuz, the miracle of the 'higher fire.'*

---

* Why did the miracle occur specifically with finding a jug of oil and revealing the higher fire, and not, for example, with finding pure Ketores, whose smoke when offered smelled like Gan Eden, as the Greeks defiled everything (not just the oil) in the Beis HaMikdash, as Chazal (Yechezkel, 7:22. *Avodah Zarah*, 52b) tell us? Because the way Hashem shows that the Shechinah rests within the Mishkan or the Beis haMikdash (which are one and the same: *Eiruvin*, 2a), is through fire. Divine Fire descended upon the Sanctuary during the dedication of the Mishkan on the eighth day: "Fire came forth from before Hashem and consumed the burnt offering on the altar" (*Vayikra*, 9:24), and during the dedication of the First Beis haMikdash ("When Shelomo finished praying, a fire descended from Heaven and consumed the burnt offerings, and the Presence of Hashem filled the Beis haMikdash" (*Divrei haYamim 2*, 7:1). Indeed, the light of the Menorah was "עדות היא לבאי עולם שהשכינה שורה בישראל /testimony to mankind that the Divine Presence rests among Israel" (*Shabbos*, 22b). This did not occur, however, with the *Chinuch* / inauguration of the Second Beis haMikdash (although the Book of Maccabees speaks of the hidden, miraculous fire from the First Beis haMikdash being revealed through Nechemyah at the dedication of the Second Beis haMikdash: *Maccabees* 2, 1:18-36, but from Chazal it is clear that we should not rely on this text, and perhaps not even read it.) With the miraculous fire of Chanukah (from the word *Chinuch*), it was 'retroactively revealed' that Hashem's Presence did rest in the Second Beis haMikdash and in the handiwork of the world 'below' (see also, *Pnei Yehoshua*, Shabbos, 21b. לכך נעשה להם ג"כ נס זה בענין הנרות שהוא עדות לישראל שהשכינה שורה בהם כדדרשי נמי לענין נר מערבי אלא שלאחר מיתת שמעון הצדיק אפילו נר מערבי לפעמים היה כבה והולך לכך נעשה להם נס בזה הענין ממש באותן הימים שהיו עת רצון להודיע שחזרו לחיבתן הראשונ). In other words, the Chanukah miracle of Heavenly Fire — much like the Heavenly Fire that was revealed during the Chinuch of the Mishkan and the First Beis haMikdash — was a confirmation that the Shechinah's presence rested in the Second Beis haMikdash just as in the First. It is also a confirmation of the *Torah she-b'al-Peh* / the oral dimension of Torah, and the human initiative from 'below', since the entire project of the Second Beis haMikdash was from 'below' Upwards.

A LIGHT WITHIN DARKNESS

'Higher fire' does not negate or consume the oil that it rests upon, nor does it negate the darkness it shines within. Both literally and metaphorically, the higher light shines within the darkness, without dispelling it completely. Light can coexist with, and shine within the darkness. In the Chanukah narrative, although the light of the Ohr haGanuz was revealed in the Beis haMikdash and burned brightly for eight long nights, the circumstances in *Yerushalayim* / Jerusalem continued to be difficult and chaotic with ongoing skirmishes and small battles. The dynasty of the Chashmona'im ended up mired in corruption, and was 'cursed', as the Rambam writes (*Bereishis*, 49:10), and, in fact, only a few hundred years later the Beis haMikdash was destroyed. Even so, their revelation of the indestructible Higher Light continued, and it continues even now. Every year, when Chanukah comes along, we are given the wonderful ability to increase the revelation of this Hidden Light, that shines within both darkness and light, this eternal light that transcends and includes all opposites, without the negation of either.

Chanukah has a unique relationship to 'darkness' and night. Most Mitzvos are performed during the day, such as putting on Tefilin or reciting a blessing on Tzitzits. Moreover, most Mitzvos of *Yomim Tovim* / Holy Days are performed during the day. We blow the Shofar on the day of Rosh Hashanah; not the night of Rosh Hashanah. We shake the Lulav and Esrog on the days of Sukkos; not on the nights of Sukkos. However, the physical Mitzvah that we perform on Chanukah is done during the evening or at night*.

* This is also true of Pesach, when the Mitzvos of the Yom Tov are mostly done by night, such as in the eating of Matzah, Maror and the Korban Pesach. (On

Why this unique distinction? Of course, technically, the miracle in the Beis haMikdash was with the oil that was burning through the night, and lighting candles during the day is superfluous. Yet, there must be a more intrinsic spiritual logic to kindling our Chanukah Menorahs in the evening.

A major, overarching theme of Chanukah, in addition to the physical battles, is the spiritual battle against the pure intellectualism of the Greeks. Pure rationalism, without a healthy sense of ethics, founded on transcendence, can lead to the greatest justifications of darkness. Indeed, וחשך / "and darkness" (*Bereishis*, 1:2) refers to the Greek Exile, and the story of Chanukah (*Medrash Rabbah*, Bereishis, 2:4. ותבא אליו היונה לעת ערב והנה עלה־זית טרף בפיה / The dove came back to him toward evening, and there in its bill was a plucked-off olive leaf": *Bereishis*, 8:11. Towards the "evening" refers to the Greek exile, and the "dove" to Klal Yisrael. Holding an olive leaf refers to the miracle with olive oil on Chanukah: *Zohar Chadash*, Noach). As the Greeks were connected with the world of darkness, thus the miracle of Chanukah and the way we celebrate Chanukah is specifically through light, and particularly through a

---

Purim we read the Megilah also by night, but the main reading is done on the next day, as are the other Mitzvos. דעיקר פרסומי ניסא הוי בקריאה דיממא: Tosefos, *Megilah*, 4a.) This is because the night of the Redemption from Egypt is a precursor for the Ultimate Redemption. Regarding the Final Redemption it says, "The light of the moon will be like the light of the sun" (*Yeshayahu*, 30:26.) A glimmer of that reality was experienced at our redemption from Egypt, as when they left Egypt in the middle of the night and yet, "The night shone like the day" (*Tehilim*, 139:12). In fact, the Torah itself calls the night of the Exodus "day": "You shall tell your children on that *day*", which certainly means the *night* of Pesach" (although *Yom* also means 'day'', as in, "It was evening, and it was light, day one"). This is the deeper reason why the Mitzvos of Pesach are done during the night rather than the day, as such a holy night *is* 'day'.

flame, as the nature of a flame of fire is to leap upwards, suggesting a yearning and longing toward the Transcendent One, 'Above'.

Kindling fire counters darkness. Therefore one would assume that the point of the lights of Chanukah is to dispel the darkness of the night, literally, metaphysically and spiritually — to replace pain and exile with light. One might also think that the Chanukah lights are similar to the candles that are lit before Shabbos. Shabbos candles are lit to enhance the ambience and light in the room; candles glowing in a dark space add *Kavod* / honor, and *Oneg* / pleasure, as we can see where we are going and enjoy what we are eating. Yet, the Mitzvah of lighting the candles on Chanukah is not utilitarian at all. They are not meant to be used for our personal pleasure or any benefit whatsoever; one may only "gaze" at them. (As the Ohr of the Menorah reaches all the way to the lower depths of reality, we refrain from any personal enjoyment from these lights, in order for there not to be a *Yenikah* / drawing of energy to the 'other side: *Pri Eitz Chayim*, 109b: 8.) In the words of the prayer following the lighting ceremony, "These lights are holy: permission is not granted to utilize them, but only to look at them." In fact, in order to avoid benefiting from these lights, another light or candle (such as the *Shamash* / extra candle used to light the Mitzvah candle) must be lit in the room, to ensure that the light of the Menorah is not what allows us to see surrounding objects.

The Chanukah lights are, in this way, a purely aesthetic or contemplative object. Meant to be appreciated, enjoyed, and engaged for what they are, rather than for what they can do. In this way, the lights of Chanukah can remind us of the inherent beauty and holiness of so many parts of the material world that we have completely translated into purely utilitarian ends, and therefore taken for granted. Chanukah comes to remind us that the Hidden Light resides within all seeming opacity, just waiting for us to kindle and appreciate its gentle glow, through a slight shift in our perception. Gazing upon the Lights of Chanukah trains our eyes to see this Hidden Light within ourselves, others, and all Creation.

Deep within the idea of Chanukah lights is the revelation of the Ohr haGanuz, and just as this Light simply exists without negation of an 'other', it can exist even within the darkness and exile. That is why the action-based Mitzvah of Chanukah is performed in the evening, in the darkness, yet not for a "purpose" such as dispelling the darkness, at least not for now. Rather these candles show how there is "light" even in the place of darkness. This is as HaKadosh Baruch Hu tells Moshe at the Burning Bush, when Moshe experienced the Ohr haGanuz, אהיה עמם בצרה זו אשר אהיה עמם בשעבוד שאר מלכיות / "'I will be' with them in this hardship, just as 'I will be' with them in their subjugation by other kingdoms," such as the Greek Exile (Rashi, *Shemos*, 3:14).

Hashem appears to Moshe precisely in the סנה / thornbush, indicating to Moshe that Hashem's Presence is present everywhere, "even in a place of thorns" (*Medrash Rabbah*, Shemos, 2:5). The thornbush remains prickly and uninviting, even as the loving Presence of Hashem is vividly resting upon it. Its 'negative' nature is not undone. Infinite Compassion and Light are there within the harsh difficulty and unclarity of exile, within all subjugations and crushing defeats, and within that which is spiritually 'prickly'.

What's more, the Ohr haGanuz reveals itself upon a dark, physical wick and crushed olive oil; it reveals itself in the darkness of night. The Ohr haGanuz is the Light of *Echad* / One, of the *Yom Echad* / Day One / the Day of Unity. This is the Light through which Adam and Chavah were able to see from one end of the world to the next; all was revealed, as all dimensions, diversity, apparent multiplicity is part of that Unity. About Day One of Creation, the day the Ohr haGanuz was created, the Torah says, "And it was ערב / *Erev* / evening, and it was בקר / *Boker* / morning, Day One." Even though there is a duality, a distinction of times, evening and morning, both are included within the One Day.

ערב / *Erev* is numerically 272. *Boker* / בקר (which is spelled as read with a Vav, as in בוקר) is 308. The difference between 272 and 308 is 36. In this way, 36 represents the hidden dimension that separates (is the "difference" between) night and day, allowing the transition from darkness to light. On a deeper level, 36 is the Ohr haGanuz that unites the evening and morning, darkness and light, and expresses itself in both evening and morning. This is the deeper reason that 'mundane' activities are permitted during Chanukah; it is an inclusion of the world of work and darkness, within the context of Divine Light. In other words, the *Ohr haGanuz* / Light of Hidden Unity is expressed within the duality of Creation. It does not undo 'work' and 'night,' nor collapse distinctions and create only light and day. Rather, it is a Light of Unity, the *Klal* / inclusive principle that is revealed within the world of mutually exclusive distinctions or *Peratim* / details.

SHEMEN / *OIL* — SHEMONAH / *EIGHT*

There is meaning in the fact that the Ohr haGanuz was revealed for eight days, and within the oil of the Menorah. The symbols of 'eight' and 'oil' are both perfect media through which the Light of

Oneness is expressed within duality, maintaining the paradox of unified opposites in this world.*

---

* It seems from *Chazal* / our sages that Shemen is connected to miracles beyond nature (beyond the paradigm of 'seven'). For example, speaking about the Shemen haMish'chah, the Gemara asks, וכי נס אחד נעשה בשמן המשחה והלא נסים הרבה נעשו בו מתחלתו ועד סופו תחלתו לא היה אלא י"ב לוג ובו נמשח המשכן וכליו ואהרן ובניו כל שבעת ימי המלואים ובו נמשחו כהנים גדולים ומלכים וכולו קיים לעתיד לבא / "And was just one miracle performed with the anointing oil? But many miracles were performed with it, from its initial preparation to its end. Its initial preparation was only the measure of twelve log, and even so the Mishkan and its vessels were anointed with it, and likewise Aaron and his sons were anointed with it all the seven days of inauguration, and High Priests and kings were anointed with it throughout the generations"; and yet despite the reduction in the amount of oil during its preparation process, as well as its multiple uses throughout history, it all remained intact for future uses: *Kerisus*, 5b. Thus, Shemen is intrinsically connected to the miraculous, and specifically to the miracles of Chanukah.

THE SEVEN LIQUIDS OF THE SEVEN HOLY DAYS: Chazal speak of seven liquids that render a food product to become ripe and thus susceptible to a status-transformation (and by means of this, to become receptive to Tumah: *Machshirim*, 6:4). These are: blood, milk, honey, dew, water, oil and wine. Liquids represent movement, fluidity, growth and transformation. These are the seven primary liquids that can help transform objects.

There are seven Yomim Tovim of the year: Rosh Hashanah, Yom Kippur, Sukkos, Chanukah, Purim, Pesach and Shavuos. These unique days placed throughout the year inspire us in different ways to self-transformation, whether through self-evaluation, liberation, receiving the Torah or calling forth genuine joy. As such, appropriately, the seven Yomim Tovim of the year are connected with these seven liquids.

Pesach is associated with ***blood***, as it is through the blood of the Korban Pesach and the blood of the Bris that we merited redemption. Blood is also a reminder of the hardship of slavery (thus Charoses is mixed with wine, as a reminder of blood: Tosefos, *Pesachim*, 116a). If possible, we drink specifically red wine for the Four Cups, to remind ourselves of, and demonstrate solidarity with, our ancestors whose blood was spilled in Egypt.

On **Shavuos**, the custom is to eat ***milk*** products. "There is a *Minhag* / custom to eat dairy foods on the first day of Shavuos, and 'a custom of Israel is Torah.' Many reasons are given": *Shulchan Aruch haRav*, Orach Chayim, 494:16.

Rosh Hashanah corresponds to ***honey***, as the custom is to dip apples in honey:

To understand this, we must first ask: Why was the miracle of Chanukah performed specifically with oil? There are many possible miracles that could have occurred as they entered the Beis haMikdash. For example, as they entered the Beis haMikdash, the *Lechem haPanim* / showbreads could have been found and miraculously remained fresh for a longer period, or they could have immediately found all the animals needed for the offerings. The answer is that the nature of Shemen is intricately connected with the entire paradigm of Chanukah.

שמן / *Shemen* / oil in Hebrew is in fact related to the word שמונה / *Shemonah* / eight. *Shemen* / oil seems to contain two paradoxical qualities. On the one hand, oil and oily, fatty foods can seep into other foods, tending to, in the language of the laws of *Ta'aruvos* / mixtures, מפעפע בכל דבר / "infiltrate all" (*Yoreh De'ah*, 105). This suggests a penetrating quality, carrying taste as it enters into spaces that normal liquids or non-oily foods would not enter nor affect to the same degree. Yet, on the other hand, the nature of oil, when mixed with other liquids, is that it rises to the top. It stays removed and detached, as it were (*Medrash Rabbah Shemos*, 36:1. *Medrash Rabbah*,

---

Tur, *Rama*, Orach Chayim, 583.
Yom Kippur is connected with ***dew***, which, like the resurrection of forgiveness, is 'a gift from Above'. Hashem accepts our Teshuvah, and states, "I will be to Israel like Dew": *Hoshea*, 14:6.
Sukkos is the time of 'judgment' for ***rain*** and ***water***: Mishnah, *Rosh Hashanah*, 16a.
Purim is connected with ***wine***, with its special Mitzvah of drinking extra wine.
Chanukah is intricately connected to ***Shemen***, as the miracle occurred with *Shemen Zayis* / ***olive oil***, and thus, even though we can light the Chanukah Menorah with anything that lights — for example a candle, since the miracle occurred with olive oil, the better way to light is with olive oil: *Darchei Moshe*.

Devarim, 7:3. See also, *Shabbos*, 5b, regarding (שמן שצף על גבי יין ונגע טבול יום בשמן).* In this way, Shemen is precisely something upon which the paradoxical Ohr haGanuz can 'reveal' itself, shining brilliantly yet not consuming, penetrating and infiltrating yet also remaining unique and detached.**

Similarly, the revelation of the Ohr haGanuz occurs for *Shemonah* / eight days and nights, as *Shemonah* alludes to paradox.

There is a world of six days, the work week, when we toil in the

---

* As such, although Shemen is not used for drink and can even be harmful (thus, when drunk alone, one does not even say a Beracha: *Shulchan Aruch*, Orach Chayim, 202:4. This also seems to be the opinion of the Rambam, *Hilchos Terumos*, 10:11, *Kesef Mishnah*, ad loc, as there is no Hana'ah. Although see, Rambam, *Hilchos Berachos*, 8:2 regarding reciting the more generic blessing of she-haKol), it can be drunk with other ingredients: *Berachos*, 35b. In other words, it stands beyond the category of an enjoyable drink. Yet, when mixed with other substances, such as beet broth, as when this mixture is used to soothe a sore throat, one *can* have *Hana'ah* /enjoyment from the oil: *Berachos*, 36a.

** The dual nature of oil (both infiltrating and remaining unique), plus its symbolism of 'wisdom', is connected to the other major theme of Chanukah, the victory of *Torah she-b'al-Peh* / the Oral Tradition of Torah wisdom over Greek wisdom. Chazal tell us (*Seder Olam Rabasi*, 1955 publishing, p. 98) that up until the point in history when Alexander the Great became Emperor, it was the time of the Prophets, and from that point forward it was the period of the Sages. In other words, the period of the rise of the Greeks, and Greek philosophy, corresponds to the end of the era of *Nevuah* / prophecy and the beginning of the period of Chazal, Torah she-b'al-Peh. Whereas Greek wisdom was related to what is merely observed with the physical senses and denied any sense of Transcendence, Torah she-b'al-Peh is the Divine Transcendent Wisdom, like oil that rises Upward to Transcendence, yet permeates everything 'below'. And in fact, it is a wisdom that is 'revealed' specifically through the 'below', the articulation of Chazal.

external realms of doing, expansion, expression, the domain of the body, and then there is a seventh day, Shabbos, the day of inwardness, being, stillness, silence, "a day of the soul", as *The Zohar* calls it (*Zohar* 2, 205b. 3, 174a). In every cycle of the week we experience both of these dimensions, the fullness and the emptiness, the *Yesh* / existence and the *Ayin* / nothingness and soul: during the six days we are in the place of Yesh and on Shabbos we inhabit Ayin.

A parallel to the seven days of the week are the seven millennia of history as we know it. Just as there are six days of the work-week and a seventh day of Shabbos, there will be six thousand years of our current historical reality, a world in which there is physical aggression, outward-directed action, material ambition, and a drive toward moving forward — and then there will be a seventh millennium, corresponding to the day of Shabbos, a time of rest and repose, reward, and presence (as Rashi writes in *Avodah Zarah*, 9a: נגזר על העולם להתקיים כמנין ימי השבוע וביום השביעי שבת ובשבעת אלפים נוח לעולם).

שית אלפי שני הוו עלמא וחד חרוב / "'Six thousand years is the duration of the world, and one thousand years in ruins.' And what does חרוב / 'ruins' mean? This refers to the time of יום שכולו שבת / when all will be Shabbos" (*Sanhedrin*, 97a). It will be a time of *Ayin* / emptiness, typified by an absence of stress, striving, competition, and active evolution.

Yesh is noise, movement, and the dense physical body. Seven is silence, stillness and the ethereal soul. In this way, 'six' is the opposite of seven; there is a tension between them, even though they ultimately complement each other.

With the coming of the seventh millennium, the Era of Moshiach will be revealed, a time of world-wide tranquility, kindness and the contemplation of Hashem's wisdom — יום שכולו שבת / a Day when all will be Shabbos. In that Era, לא יהיה שם לא רעב ולא מלחמה. ולא קנאה ותחרות. שהטובה תהיה משפעת הרבה. וכל המעדנים מצויין כעפר. ולא יהיה עסק כל העולם אלא לדעת את ה' בלבד / "there will be no famine, no war, no envy and no competition. For the good will be very pervasive. All the delicacies will be as readily available as is dust. The world will only be engaged in knowing Hashem" (Rambam, *Hilchos Melachim*, 12:5).

After the period of the Seventh Millennium, the time of ימות המשיח / the Days of Moshiach, will come an Eighth Millennium, the time of עולם הבא / *Olam haBa* / the World to Come. *Olam haBa* is a time of the resurrection of the body, of all bodies that have lived and are no longer among the living (Ramban, *Toras haAdam*, Sha'ar haG'mul. *Targum Yonoson*, Yeshayahu, 58:11, *Emunos veDeyos*, 7:5. Ra'avad, *Hilchos Teshuvah*, 8:2. *Derashos haRan*, 5, although the Rambam maintains that Olam haBa comes 'after' the resurrection. *Hilchos Teshuvah*, 8:2. *Igeres Techiyas haMeisim*, 4. See also, *Chovos haLevavos*, 4:4. *Kuzari*, 1:115. *Sefer haIkarim*, 4:30-33). Whereas the Seventh Millennium is a time of transcendence, tranquility and Ayin, the Eighth Millennium is once again about the body and the physical world. In other words, 'eight' represents the 'inclusive transcendence', the inclusion of soul and body, the 'six' and the 'seven', Yesh *and* Ayin, dark and light. Hence the symbolic significance of the light of Chanukah, the Higher Fire of spirituality that rests upon but does not dualistically oppose or seek to subdue the body, the physical wick upon which it resides.

'Eight' can be viewed as the number that simply comes *after* 'seven', and thus it can represent a *lower* dimension than 'seven' and its quality of transcendence. On the other hand, 'eight' can also be the first number of a higher order of numbers and dimensions, the higher unity of inclusive transcendence — eight as a reality that comes *'before'* seven.* This is eight as the original unity of six and seven, before the Tree of Dualistic Knowledge. Chanukah embodies the quality of eight that is of a higher order, beyond the realm of six and seven, eight 'before' seven, and yet it includes and permeates the opposing realms of six and seven within its expansive embrace.* The nature of the *Shemen* / oil of Chanukah is that it both floats above and permeates below. The nature of the *Shemonah* / eight days of Chanukah is that it both transcends darkness, like the 'Seventh' Day and permeates the darkness of the 'six' days. It is both 'high' and 'low' at the same time.

Chanukah is where the dimension of 'eight' flows into the dimension of 'seven', similar to what the Mishnah says (*Yuma*, 5:4) regarding the eight sprinklings of the blood on the *Mizbeach* / altar:

* This idea of the 'eight that comes before the seven' is reflected in an interesting *Din* / law of Chanukah. The Gemara (*Shabbos*, 21b) writes that the Mitzvah to light Chanukah lights is משתשקע החמה עד שתכלה רגל מן השוק / "from when the sun sinks down until traffic in the marketplace ceases". The term משתשקע / sinks means after *Sh'kia*, the end of sunset, when the orb of the sun has 'sunk' completely below the horizon, as the Shulchan Aruch rules (אין מדליקין נר חנוכה קודם שתשקע החמה: *Orach Chayim*, 672:1 — מצותה מסוף שקיעת החמה). Yet, the Rambam writes, אלא עם שקיעתה לא מאחרין ולא מקדימין / "(It is) *with* the sunset, not later or earlier: *Hilchos Megilah v'Chanukah*, 4:5. This seems puzzling, as the 25th of Kislev proper only begins once the sun has fully set and it is dark, many minutes after *Sh'kia*. According to the Rambam's timing, on the first night of Chanukah, we would be lighting the Menorah on what is technically the 24th of Kislev. This is especially troubling since הדלקה עושה מצוה / "the act of lighting accomplishes the Mitzvah," as opposed to the light which may continue to burn into the night. The deeper answer is because Chanukah represents the Eight that comes before the seven, or the *Achas v'Achas, Achas v'Shtayim....*

the Kohen Gadol would count, אחת, אחת ואחת, אחת ושתים, אחת ושלש, אחת וארבע, אחת וחמש, אחת ושש, אחת ושבע / "*Achas* / One. One and one, one and two, one and three, one and four, one and five, one and six, one and seven." The first "one" that precedes the count of seven is really the 'eighth' count, 'above' and 'before' the seven. And yet, "one" also permeates each of the seven counts.*

This is the idea of the higher, more transcendent and more inclusive 'eight', alluding to the Ohr haGanuz, which maintains paradox, in a seamless simultaneity of existence and non-existence, light and darkness, rest and work, stillness and movement, silence and noise, soul and body, Ayin and Yesh, redemption and exile.**

EVEN IN EXILE

This paradoxical nature is found also in the military victory of the Chashmona'im.

In the story of Chanukah, the Chashmona'im regained control over the Beis haMikdash and only parts of Yerushalayim, but did not throw off the yoke of the Greek-Assyrian rule completely, and, as

* Shemen is not *Sovea* / 'satisfying' (as in *Sheva* / seven). Yet, "...The olive tree replied, 'Have I, through whom G-d and men are honored, stopped yielding my rich oil?'"(*Shoftim*, 9:9) Shemen is rich and fatty and saturates everything. In other words, it stands apart from the 'seven', yet it permeates the seven.

** "The light was hidden away for the Future..." (for the ultimate purpose and culmination of history). Shemen is connected to *Kavod* / honor (ויאמר להם הזית החדלתי את־דשני אשר־בי יכבדו...*Shoftim*, 9:9), and Kavod is the objective of Creation — כל מה שברא הקדוש ברוך הוא בעולמו, לא בראו אלא לכבודו (*Avos*, 6:11). Thus Kavod is the *Tachlis* / purpose and the *Rosh* / headquarters or principal intention of Creation. This principal intention is connected to the idea of Shemen as well, as oil rises up and yet permeates. It is the *Achas* / One that permeates all the 'seven', i.e., the natural world.

mentioned, the house of the Chashmona'im did not end well. One might ask, why celebrate a minor miracle that seems not to have had a widespread or lasting effect on the world and Jewish history? We celebrate it because an even deeper level of the Ohr haGanuz has been revealed to us, conveying the promise that Hashem will be with us *in* our exiles and dark times, not just *after* them. At the Burning Bush, HaKadosh Baruch Hu reveals the Name Ehe'yeh, saying to Moshe, 'I am with them now, and will be with them in their next exile, I will always be with them.' HaKadosh Baruch Hu does *not* say, 'I will ensure there is no exile, as I cannot coexist with exile.' Rather, Hashem says, 'I will be with them *in* their exile. I am the Light that is always present, always tolerating, never consuming, even allowing exile (for the time being).'

In the liturgy of Chanukah we say, ולך עשית שם גדול וקדוש בעולמך / "...For Yourself You made a great and holy Name in Your world." What does "a great Name" mean? What is גדול / great? Our sages tell us, בכל מקום שאתה מוצא גדולתו של הקב"ה, שם אתה מוצא ענוותנותו / "Wherever we find the Greatness of the Holy One, Blessed be He, you also find His humility" (*Megaleh Amukos*, 1791. See *Megilah*, 31a). The deepest definition of "great" is HaKadosh Baruch Hu's quality of being humble and tolerant to the point of not overwhelming existence. Great means to be humble, to allow, to gently inspire without overpowering. We sense greatness when a powerful person does not make us feel smaller, but rather, makes us feel great as well. On Chanukah this great Light, the Ohr haGanuz, was revealed to Klal Yisrael in the form of a more 'modern' version of the Burning Bush: a small, discarded jug of hand-crushed oil and a humble, perhaps makeshift candelabrum, upon which rested the all-glorious Light of Creation in a most gentle way, not even consuming the oil.

CHANUKAH: THE 'LOWEST' AND 'HIGHEST' HOLY DAY

As explored, Chanukah is connected with the idea of eight, with Shemen, and with the idea of unifying Transcendence with immanence — the unity between Yesh and Ayin, Shabbos and weekday, holy and mundane. All of this is also associated with Chanukah being an expression of the eighth Sefirah, *Hod* / Splendor, the lowest of the emotional Sefiros. On the one hand, Chanukah is the 'lowest' Yom Tov that is connected with a lower Sefira (the three Yomim Tovim that are *Min haTorah* / explicitly described in Tanach, correspond to the three higher emotional Sefiros, Chesed, Gevurah and Tiferes). On the other hand, like a flame, Chanukah 'leaps' higher than its basic category and is thus connected with the higher Sefirah of Netzach as well.

In general, Chanukah and Purim correspond to the Sefiros of Hod and Netzach, respectively (*Pri Eitz Chayim*, Sha'ar Purim, 6. Elsewhere it is written the opposite, that Chanukah is Netzach and Purim is Hod: *Pri Eitz Chayim*, Derush Chag haShavuos, towards the end. Maharam miPanu, *Mein Ganim*, Seder haMoadim, 15d. The Ramak brings both opinions as well: *Ohr Yakar* on Tikunei Zohar, vol. 1, 12b. Perhaps Chanukah is in Netzach, yet its Tikun is in Hod: Ramchal, *Kitzur haKavanos*, Inyan Chanukah). The inner qualities of Hod are submission and praise, while Netzach is victory and exaltation. Chanukah is a time to offer *Hoda'ah* / praise, and Purim is more an explosion of triumphant ecstasy. Purim is also a louder, noisier Holy Day, in the mode of the outward-oriented Sefirah of

Netzach, while Chanukah is a gentler, quieter, more introspective Holy Day, a time of lighting a small flame and humbly singing praises.

As corresponding to the three principle emotive Sefiros, the *Shalosh Regalim* / Torah-based Yomim Tovim are Pesach / Chesed (Avraham), Shavuos / Gevurah (Yitzchak), and Sukkos / Tiferes (Yaakov). The Rabbinic Yomim Tovim are of the lower Sefiros, which are 'external' or outwardly oriented.*

What does this mean? Hashem's *Chesed* / kindness is revealed through *Yetzias Mitzrayim* / the Exodus from Egypt and the Yom Tov of Pesach. Hashem's *Gevurah* / power is revealed through

* Purim is not even celebrated with the recitation of Half Hallel, however Chanukah is celebrated with the Full Hallel, as if it were one of the *Shalosh Regalim* / Three Pilgrimage Festivals. Indeed, Chanukah is also called a *Moed* / Holy Day: *Tikkunei Zohar*, Chadash, p. 58b — and it is even called a *Regel* / Pilgrimage Festival: *Pri Eitz Chayim*, 109c. Thus the Gemara says "*HaRagil b'Ner* / if someone is *Ragil* / 'accustomed' to using candles…": *Shabbos*, 23. The reason the term that is used is *Ragil* (unlike *Zahir*, which Chazal, ad loc, write regarding Mezuzah) is to hint that Chanukah is a *Regel*: *Degel Machaneh Ephrayim*, Chanukah.

Regel, in numerical value, is 233. This is the value of the Name Havayah and Ehe'yeh filled, or spelled out, using the letter Yud (*Sha'ar haKavanos*, Kavanos haTevilah Erev Yom Tov, p. 78a):

Yud (Yud/10, Vav/6, Dalet/4 = 20) **Hei** (Hei/5, Yud/10 = 15) **Vav** (Vav/6, Yud/10, Vav/6 = 22). **Hei** (Hei/5, Yud /10 = 15) in total is **72.**

Ehe'yeh is spelled out as **Aleph** (Aleph/1, Lamed/30, Pei/80 = 111) **Hei** (Hei/5, Yud/10 = 15) **Yud** (Yud/10, Vav/6, Dalet/4 = 20) **Hei** (Hei/5, Yud/10 = 15) in total is **161**.

72 + 161 = **233.**

The filling of these Names with the letter Yud is significant, as Yud is the channel of Divine *Chochmah* / wisdom. The whole internal battle between the Greeks and Klal Yisrael is about the Divine nature of Chochmah.

the Giving of the Torah and the Yom Tov of Shavuos. Hashem's Tiferes is revealed in shelter of the Clouds of Glory and the Yom Tov of Sukkos. On the 'lower' level, Hashem's *Netzach* / eternal victory is revealed through the Rabbinic Holy Day of Purim. And even lower, Hashem's *Hod* / humble splendor is revealed through the Rabbinic Holy Day of Chanukah. Chanukah is the 'lowest', but in a way it is also the highest, in that Hashem's revelation is revealed within the lowest, darkest level. This resonates with the pattern discussed above: 'eight' representing both the world below and the higher, transcendent realms.

Netzach and Hod are also connected with both active and passive Bitachon. Although Chanukah is intricately woven with the idea of Hod, there is also an opinion that it is connected to Netzach (The Ramak, *Ohr Yakar*, on Tikkunei Zohar, 1, 12b, brings down both opinions: Chanukah is Hod or Netzach and Purim is Netzach or Hod). There are two opinions on where to put the Menorah if one is lighting in the home (*Shabbos*, 22a): either the Menorah is placed on the right side of the door, or the left side of the door (the latter is the Halachah). The argument is based on whether the main point of Chanukah corresponds to Netzach or Hod. Netzach, referring to the victory of the battle, is a right side Sefirah. The Cohanim are from Chesed, which is also on the right side, and the miracle was with oil, which is a depiction of Divine Chochmah, another right side Sefirah. However, the Halachah follows the main point of Chanukah, which is that Matisyahu made a *Tikun* / rectification on the *Midah* / attribute of Hod, a left side Sefirah. There was indeed a *Netzach* / triumph in the Chanukah narrative, but we celebrate it in the mode of Hod — Hallel and Hoda'ah. Thus the Menorah is placed on the left side. In the same way that it is necessary to balance Gevurah and Din with Chesed, so as not to become rigidly judgmental and harsh, it is spiritually essential to couch any experience of Netzach, victory, within the context of Hod, grateful acknowledgment of Hashem's presence and blessing, so as not to become too full of ourselves.

There is a mode of *Mesiras Nefesh* / self-sacrifice which corresponds to each Midah. For example, a person can have Mesiras Nefesh in the mode of the Midah of Chochmah, and transcend their limitations through Torah study. A person can have Mesiras Nefesh to reveal Hashem's Netzach and victoriously overcome all of their doubt and negativity. Matisyahu and the Maccabees had Mesiras Nefesh to reveal the Hod, the glory of Hashem in this 'lowest' world.* This produced a rectification that still shines today, no matter how dark our times may seem. Only the highest of Holy Days could accomplish this, a day of the 'higher (hidden) fire'.

* Mesiras Nefesh means to go beyond oneself, beyond one's comfort zone. Therefore, when a person has Mesiras Nefesh in the expression of any specific Midah, for example, going beyond their seeming limits in giving and doing Chesed, their Mesiras Nefesh includes all the others Midos as well (in this example, the person also goes beyond their comfort zone in *Gevurah* / Strength, etc.) As such, his and the Maccabees Mesiras Nefesh for the Kavod and Hod of Hakadush Baruch Hu, and by extension of all of Klal Yisrael, allowed them to tap into the Divine Sefirah of Hod — but through the Mesiras Nefesh itself they also connected with *Netzach* / Victory (and all of the other Sefiros) and were victorious.

CONNECTING TO THE OHR HAGANUZ IN AVODAH

To review, the Ohr haGanuz is the Light of Unity that is expressed in all the dualities of Creation, such as light and darkness, evening and morning, redemption and exile. Paradoxically, this Light does not erase the world of distinctions and impose only light and redemption, rather, it is revealed within the world of distinctions. In our own personal *Avodah* / spiritual consciousness and inner work, this means that the miracle of Chanukah reveals that "we are servants of Hashem (connected) in a manifest manner even within the darkness" (*Sefas Emes,* Chanukah, 5632). This light, the most hidden, deepest light within our souls does not necessarily or immediately negate the darkness in our lives. Eventually all our darkness will be illumined, but while we are in-process as human beings, we are connected to HaKadosh Baruch Hu's Light even when we are still within a condition of personal and collective darkness. This is much like the literal story of the oil, which glowed brightly although it did not consume the wick or oil, and the fact that the spiritual light of Chanukah did not dispel the darkness and coarseness of the Greeks altogether. The Ohr haGanuz reveals to us that HaKadosh Baruch Hu's Presence is with us even in this thorny exile, in the *Peratim* / details of our often chaotic lives. Our Avodah is thus to sense this deepest truth, that wherever we may be Hashem is always with us, and to take all the apparent dualities of life, all the Peratim, and draw them back into the Klal, the Oneness of Hashem.

LIGHT OF INSPIRATION

During our exile, this is our Avodah throughout the entire year, and especially during the darker and more challenging periods of our lives, in our own times of 'winter solstice', when it feels cold, dark, and uninviting: to know that even here is the Presence and Light of Hashem, and that specifically here we can serve Hashem in the deepest way.

It is quite common for people to be inspired when confronted with a challenge, and with everything they can muster, triumphantly rise to the occasion. In these moments, their inner 'oil' of purity is awakened and it shines brightly. Unfortunately, however, these peak moments can be mere temporary flashes of inspiration. When the high is over, many people sadly plummet back to their center of gravity in the smaller self.

Each day of the week brings a different shade of experience. Some of us experience spiritual inspiration and ease on Shabbos, while Friday is full of intense effort. Some feel relaxed and happy on Sundays, but tense and unhappy on Mondays. Part of the miracle of Chanukah was that the Chashmona'im were able to kindle the Menorah for eight consecutive nights. As mentioned, the 'vessel' that engendered, drew down and maintained the miracle of the oil and the Light was their *Bitachon* / trust, their determination, focus and hope. The Chashmona'im kept up this inspiration, Bitachon and faith for eight days — extending beyond the natural cycle of the week. If Chanukah began on Sunday Night, the last night was again Sunday Night, and yet they were still inspired as if it was the first night, possibly even more so. Because their 'vessels' were in place for eight long nights, the miracle extended for eight nights, which transcends the natural cycle of seven and intimates a taste of eternity in the present moment.

The following year, the sages realized that the inspiration and light that was revealed on Chanukah had not died out. It was timeless. Thus they established Chanukah as a Yom Tov for all generations and all time.

Unlike all Torah-based Holy Days, at the end of Chanukah there is no Havdalah or 'separation' service. Halachically, we do not recite Havdalah at the end of Chanukah because it is merely a Rabbinic Yom Tov. Yet, the deeper reason for this is that the Bitachon and light of Chanukah is really available throughout the year. The light of Chanukah is thus not separate from any condition or experience and can potentially be accessed any day of the year. In other words, it is endless.

TRUST, INNER LIGHT & DREAMS

To recap, Kislev is a month connected with peaceful, 'trustful' sleep and dreams. Through reawakening our Bitachon, our *Kesel* / trust in HaKadosh Baruch Hu, we tap into, reveal and unleash the *Lamed Vav* / the Thirty Six Lights of the Ohr haGanuz. This Light is forever present within us, deep within all experience and all Creation.

Bitachon, with the inner strength and holy confidence it brings, is the *Kli* / vessel that receives and taps into miracles. In Kislev, as the darkest night of the year approaches, around the time of the winter solstice, we celebrate by kindling lights and thanking Hashem for the miracles of Chanukah, and for all our past. At this time, as we fill our hearts with praise and gratefulness, Bitachon and conviction, we are able to rekindle our dreams and aspirations. During these auspicious days, when the cosmic *Shefa* / flow of miracles is opened through our Bitachon, much like that of the Chashmona'im, we open ourselves up for miracles to be revealed in our lives, even in those places we might least expect.

Yet, often, in order for us to truly open ourselves up for the possibility of something radically new and miraculous to occur, we need to first 'go to sleep' (as the sense of the month indicates) from our past, and let go of what we are holding onto. Simply, we need to let go of the old, whatever our limited mind conjures up and grasps, and allow for the possibility of something wonderfully unexpected. Let us say, for example, you are looking for a new job and you had an interview and you are *Davening* / praying that they accept your resume. To allow your Bitachon to open you to HaKadosh Baruch Hu's miracles you need to "go to sleep" from your perception of what you think you need, i.e.: this particular job. You need to have Bitachon for something bigger, to dream and pray and make a vessel for it.

HaKadosh Baruch Hu is Infinite and there are infinite possibilities* in this Divine Creation; we should not place HaKadosh Baruch Hu within our conceptual limits, so to speak.

---

* The Ohr haGanuz is connected with the Olam haMalbush: *Emek haMelech*, Sha'ar 13:15. Olam haMalbush is the inner dimension and highest, deepest reality of the Letters of Creation, the building blocks of Creation, composed of the 231 possible letter combinations. In essence, Olam haMalbush is the potential of all possibilities.

SUMMARY OF KISLEV

KISLEV COMES IN THE COLDEST SEASON, AND CONTAINS the darkest week of the year, when the moon is waning leading up to the winter solstice, stimulating us to create the light and warmth of fire, the **element** of the month. This represents an 'awakening from below', as indicated by the **name** of the month, alluding to *Kislam* / 'their trust'. When we awaken trust, no matter how dark our circumstances, we create the vessels for the light of miracles. This is hinted at in the **letter sequence of Hashem's name** for this month, in which the 'upper' letters (hidden Divine lights) flow into the 'lower' letters (receptive vessels). Chanukah, the **Yom Tov** of the month, is a revelation of the *Ohr haGanuz* / Hidden Divine Light within the vessels of humble trust.

Of the **body parts** associated with this month are the *Kesel* / loins, embodying *Bitachon* / trust. Samach, the **letter** of the month, means 'support', and just as the loins are vessels that support the whole upper body, Bitachon is the support and basis for our spiritual life in this world.

Bitachon is also necessary to relax and release one's anxieties in order to achieve sound 'sleep', the **sense** of the month. The **Torah portions** read during this month frequently reference sleep and miraculous dreams. The **sign** of the month is *Keshes* / bow. As drawing the arrow back allows it to fly, trustingly descending into the darkness of sleep allows us to awaken with strength and live a life of Bitachon and Hoda'ah.

The **tribe** of the month, Binyamin alludes to the Chanukah miracle which occurred in Yerushalayim, the portion of Eretz Yisrael allocated to the tribe of Binyamin. Yerushalayim was and will be the location of the revelation of the Ohr haGanuz, in the Beis ha-Mikdash. The **verse** of the month speaks of the burial of Yaakov. The Medrash reveals that his coffin was adorned with 36 spiritual crowns, corresponding to the 36 lights of Chanukah, and the 36 hours that the Ohr haGanuz shone in Gan Eden, and which will shine in the coming Complete Redemption.

12 DIMENSIONS OF KISLEV	
Sequence of Hashem's Name	*Vav-Yud-Hei-Hei (he 'masculine' letters followed by the 'feminine' letters)*
Torah Verse	*VaYar Yoshev haAretz haKenaani / and the settlers of Canaan saw…" (Bereishis, 50:11)*
Letter	*Samach (support)*
Month Name	*Alludes to Kislam / 'their trust'*
Sense	*Sleep*
Zodiac	*Keshes / the Bow, or Kashos / the Archer; Sagittarius*
Tribe	*Binyamin / Benjamin*
Body Part	*Keiva / stomach or Kesel / loins*
Element	*Fire*
Parshios / Torah Portions	*Toldos through VaYeshev and sometimes Miketz; sleep and dreams*
Season	*Darkest week of the year*
Holy Day	*Chanukah*

PRACTICE
Gratitude and Thankfulness

THE DAYS OF CHANUKAH ARE CALLED THE DAYS OF הלל והודאה / *Hallel v'Hoda'ah* / praise and thanksgiving. Hallel and Hoda'ah are intricately bound with Chanukah, so much so that the Rambam chose to enfold the laws of Hallel within his elucidation of the Laws of Chanukah.

Bitachon / trust is one essential ingredient we need in order to tap into the miraculous; we also need Hallel and Hoda'ah. In fact, these two perspectives inspire and reinforce one another. After recording the events of the first Chanukah miracle, our sages conclude, "The following year, *these days* were appointed as a Yom Tov to sing praise and offer thanks." In other words, in order that these miracles be revealed in our own days ("these days") we need the vessel of Hoda'ah to HaKadosh Baruch Hu for all the gifts we have received in the past and are receiving in the present. To assimilate and carry forward these miracles we need Bitachon in the future.

Every year, particularly during the Chanukah period, there is a heightened potential for revealed miracles, much like the miracles that occurred on the first Chanukah. Yet, as the sages teach, to truly tap into this potential we first need to be grateful and thankful to Hashem for all of the collective and personal miracles that have already happened. This is a miraculous time, we just need to ensure that we ourselves live 'miraculously' — with *Emunah* / faith and Bitachon and abundant expressions of gratitude, thereby creating the vessel that draws down the revelation of miracles into our lives.

We should always be "singing praise and offering thanks"; we should never cease enumerating our thanks for all the life, health, joy and friendship that Hashem has given us, and gives us every moment. This is always the case, in every month and day of the year. However, it is vital to strongly emphasize it during Kislev, a time of heavy darkness and heightened potential for miracles.

It is brought down in the name of Tzadikim that a *Segulah* / auspicious act, for meriting to see real miracles in our lives is to refrain from complaining during the entire month of Kislev and through the end of Chanukah. If you find yourself complaining, simply pause and insert an expression of gratitude instead; aspire to sing praise and thank Hashem for all the continuous gifts of life.

ALWAYS BE GRATEFUL

כל הנשמה תהלל / "Let all that breathes praise..." (*Tehilim*, 150:6), according to the Medrash (*Bereishis Rabbah,* 14:9), על כל נשימה ונשימה שאדם נושם צריך לקלס לבורא / "with every 'breath and breath' that a person breathes they should praise the Creator." In fact, we are naturally offering HaKadosh Baruch Hu praise with every breath, so-to-speak, though this has to become a conscious and active process for it to draw down inner growth and revealed blessings. We must first become aware of the implicit reality in order to harness and amplify its potential through explicit expression.

We ought to be grateful and thankful every single moment we are alive, for to praise and sing of Hashem's unity is the very purpose our mouths were created. להודות לך / "to offer praise to You", this is the very reason we have a mouth (שהפה נברא להודות לה' וליחדו. *Kaf haChayim*, Orach Chayim, 60:4, in the name of the Arizal. Chida, *Midbar Kadmos*, Zayin). Indeed "כל המרבה להודות את ה' ולשבחו תמיד הרי זה משבח / the more one thanks Hashem and offers praise, the more praiseworthy one is" (Rambam, *Hilchos Berachos*, 10:26).

Our sages say, הקורא הלל בכל יום הרי זה מחרף ומגדף / "One who reads Hallel every day (is tantamount) to one who curses and blasphemes (Hashem)" (*Shabbos*, 118b). This is because when we recite Hallel, meaning here the specific chapters in Tehilim which speak about the miraculous Exodus from Egypt, we are focusing on supernatural, extraordinary events. If we were to do this every day, it would seem that we are dismissing the deeper miracles vested within nature, and the miracle of nature itself (*Kesav Sofer*, Vayetze, 29:35). On the other hand, the transcendent miracles of the Torah are given to show us that there is actually no absoluteness to nature, meaning that *everything* in life, in nature, is miraculous, wonderful, and Divinely orchestrated (Ramban, *Shemos*, 13:16. ומן הנסים הגדולים המפורסמים אדם מודה בנסים הנסתרים שהם יסוד התורה כלה, שאין לאדם חלק בתורת משה רבינו עד שנאמין בכל דברינו ומקרינו שכלם נסים אין בהם טבע ומנהגו של עולם, בין ברבים בין ביחיד, אלא אם יעשה המצות יצליחנו שכרו, ואם יעבור עליהם יכריתנו ענשו, הכל בגזרת עליון). Not only can we, but we should always aspire to be in a posture of gratefulness and thanksgiving, every moment of the day — for the continuous miracles 'within nature', for life itself and all its gifts. The revealed light of a given miracle takes us beyond the world, so to speak, while the hidden light of Chanukah brings us back into the world, but now with the light of the Holy One before us.

King Shlomo says, איש לפי מהללו / "And a man is tested by his praise" (*Mishlei*, 27:21). The simple meaning of this teaching is that every person is known and tested by how other people praise him. Yet, Rabbeinu Yonah writes that this means you can know a man by what he praises and what he thinks to praise (איש לפי מהללו מפירוש מעלות האדם לפי מה שיהלל. אם הוא משבח המעשים והטובים והחכמים והצדיקים תדע ובחנת כי איש טוב הוא ושרש הצדק נמצא בו: *Sha'arei Teshuvah*, 3:148).

SHOWING GRATITUDE IN ACTION: BEYOND THE LETTER OF THE LAW

Upon reflection, it becomes clear that there is something quite unique about the miraculous experience that occurred in the Chanukah story, compared to the other miracles recorded and celebrated as Holy Days. The Chanukah miracle occurs *after* the salvation and is not the cause or catalyst of the redemption. This is unlike, for example, Pesach, when the miraculous plagues forced the reluctant Pharaoh to send the Jews out of Egypt. It is unlike Purim, when Ester 'miraculously' became the queen and the favorite wife of Achashverosh, allowing her to annul the decree initiated by Haman. On Chanukah, the Chashmona'im were first victorious in battle, and then *after* the fact, a miracle occurred with the oil. It seems this miracle was a kind of Divine confirmation of the salvation that had already happened — there seems to be no other reason for the miracle.

As a Divine confirmation, the miracle of the oil reinforces the idea of HaKadosh Baruch Hu's unconditional and unbridled love for us: לכך נראה דעיקר הנס לא נעשה אלא להודיע להם חיבת המקום עליהם / "It appears that essentially, the miracle was made in order to cause them to know the affection of the Omnipresent for them" (*Pnei Yehoshua*, Shabbos, 21b). A Divine confirmation inspired the building of the Second Beis haMikdash, as well. A Heavenly fire descended, showing that the Shechinah was present there, much like the fire that descended during the inaugurations of the Mishkan and the First Beis haMikdash. These events also demonstrated Hashem's ongoing unconditional commitment to our covenant.

Part of the miracle is that they found pure oil when it was completely unlikely that any was left in such circumstance. And in truth, they could have used impure oil to light the Menorah. There is a principle that טומאה הותרה בציבור / laws of impurity are not only דחוייה / pushed aside when the entire community is impure, rather they are הותרה / permitted. Impure oil was thus permissible for the Menorah in this particular instance (*Pnei Yehoshua* on Shabbos, 21b: ולכאורה יש לתמוה כל טורח הנס זה למה דהא קי"ל טומאה הותרה בציבור והיו יכולין להדליק בשמן

טמא ובשלמא למ"ד דחויה בציבור ניחא הכא שפיר קצת משא"כ למ"ד הותרה בציבור). But it seemed HaKadosh Baruch Hu was already going "beyond the letter of the law" with us, showing affectionate commitment beyond the natural order, giving us a gift and a sign that He knew would bring us great joy. Beyond all expectation, here was a jug of pure oil, just asking to be lit in service of the Creator.

As a response to this Divine generosity, on Chanukah we gratefully show our commitment to HaKadosh Baruch Hu. Unlike with other Mitzvos for which many people look to follow the most lenient of opinions, exemptions and loopholes, on Chanukah we all go beyond the letter of the law, as the Mitzvah is for one person to light one candle each night for the entire household (*Shabbos*, 21b). Yet, we all light the Menorah, and in addition we increase in the number of lights with every passing day, engaging in a *Hiddur* of a *Hiddur* / an extra, affectionate 'beautification' of the Mitzvah. (This Hiddur is actually part of the *Takanah* / edict to light Chanukah candles itself. In general, performing a Hiddur Mitzvah is limited to *Ad Shelish* / up until a third of the price above the basic cost of the Mitzvah: *Baba Kama*, 9b. For example, "If one find two Esrogim for sale and one is nicer than the other, he should spend up to a third extra for the nicer Esrog" *Shulchan Aruch*, Orach Chayim, 656, whereas with Chanukah, for the Hiddur, one can spend even more than a Shelish). Indeed this has become the common practice, even though it is far beyond the letter of the law and was once merely a custom of those who wanted to do more than the obligatory. By creating a Hiddur, we express our overflowing gratitude in a concrete way by doing something 'extra' for our Benefactor. We send a gift and a sign of love and gratitude back to our Beloved.

MODEH ANI / *The Thanking I*

There are various practices that can help us inspire and cultivate a posture of gratefulness. One way is simply to continuously ask yourself: What are the extraordinary miracles of my life? What are the so-called ordinary gifts in my life? And then think and ask yourself: 'How can I express my thanks and appreciation — through thought, word and action — for these beautiful gifts?'

We need to think this way throughout the entire day. Certainly, upon awakening each day and throughout the beginning of the day, this should be a foundational thought and expression. In fact, the Baal Shem Tov teaches that all our words articulated throughout the day are predicated on the first words we utter upon awakening. If our thoughts and words are infused with gratefulness and thankfulness, then all our thoughts and words will follow suit the entire day.

A mere reflection on our life's myriad blessings upon awakening can induce a deep and lasting posture of gratefulness. In truth, every morning when we awake, a small miracle occurs. Sleep is a minor form of death and when we wake up refreshed, rejuvenated and revived, we have experienced a glimmer of 'resurrection'. Every morning our soul and vitality is 'returned' to us. At night as we retire to bed we give our soul over to its Maker, as it were. We let go and die a little bit, hence we say the Shema right before falling asleep, as we are bidden to do on our 'deathbed'. Every morning as we awaken, our soul is returned to us. To mark this 'small miracle' among all the miracles of life, we declare the *Modeh Ani* / "I am grateful," prayer.

First appearing in the 1500's, the *Modeh Ani* prayer is composed, or at least recorded, by Rav Moshe Ibn Machir in *Seder haYom.* It is a Tefilah of thanksgiving that we recite the first moment we realize we are awake:

Modeh Ani — I offer thanks

L'fanecha — to You

Melech Chai v'Kayam — Living and Eternal King

Shehe-che-zarta — for you have restored

Bi — within me

Nishmasi — my soul

B'Chemla — with mercy.

Raba Emunasecha — Great is Your faith (in me)*

Instead of waking up in the morning and feeling our 'I', as in, "I am so tired," or "did I sleep enough," or "I have so much to do today," we open our eyes and offer our first words and thoughts to the Master of the Universe, in gratitude for giving us the gift of a new day. This consciousness forms a foundation for the rest of the day.

As we recite these words of acknowledgement, we become acutely aware that our lives are lived in the Presence of the Master

* *Yerushalmi, Berachos* 4:1, writes that when you wake up in the morning you should say מודה אני לפניך ה׳ אלוקי ואלוקי אבותי שהוצאתני מאפילה לאורה / "I offer thanks to You, Hashem my G-d and the G-d of my ancestors, who has taken me out from darkness to light." And in the afternoon we should offer thanks for being able to see the sun in the east in the morning, and now setting in the west.

of the Universe, that we are always *L'fanecha* / 'in front of You'. And we are deeply humbled by the faith and confidence that Hashem has in us, returning our soul to us, investing in us, and giving us another day. With daily repetition of the Modeh Ani with conscious *Kavanah* / intention, we gradually build up a strong foundation of humble gratitude.

We also develop deeper levels of Bitachon in this practice. When we recognize that *Raba Emunasecha* / "Great is Your faith [in us]", our faith in HaKadosh Baruch Hu is stimulated in response. Great is the Divine faithfulness through which our soul and vitality is returned to us; in doing so, our Creator demonstrates great faith in us. We are entrusted with another day in which to serve HaKadosh Baruch Hu. We are trusted to add to the Light in this world. When we sense that our Creator trusts us, we too begin to trust the Creator and ourselves. And the more Bitachon we have, the more we can draw down miracles into our lives. Much like Chashmona'im, we will have a strong vessel of Bitachon, which empowers us to search for and find the Light of miracles.

Modeh Ani is an eminently powerful passage that transmits both the humility of gratitude and faith, and simultaneously our own inner greatness, in the fact that the Master of the Universe has faith in us and our potential. We can root our day in this paradox of being in a state of *Modeh* / surrender, which is *Bitul* / transparency of the egoic 'I', and the genuine empowerment of recognizing Hashem's faith in us, and thereby we can accomplish our mission and purpose for the coming day. For this reason, it is no wonder that the Rebbe זצוק"ל נ"ע, chose to explore the essence of Chassidus, which is the unity of *Ayin* / non-thingness and the Ultimate

Yesh / existence, through a discussion of this prayer. A young boy once asked the Rebbe's mother, Rebbetzin Chanah, what her son's favorite Tefilah was. "I do not know, but I will ask him," she replied. The next time the young boy met the Rebbetzin, she told him: *Modeh Ani.*

KAVANAH / MINDFUL INTENTION

Part of having faith and Bitachon in Hashem is having trust and Bitachon in yourself. *Raba Emunasecha* / "Great is Your faith": we have faith in HaKadosh Baruch Hu who has great faith in us. When the Torah says, following the Splitting of the Sea, "And they believed in Hashem and in Moshe his servant," this, say the Chassidic Rebbes, means they believed in Hashem *and in themselves* — Moshe is a code word for the entire nation, being the heart and soul of the People. They had Emunah and Bitachon not only that Hashem performs miracles, they also had *Bitachon Atzmi* / self-confidence and self-trust that they were worthy of receiving miracles.

Trusting and believing in yourself and your potential comes from the realization that the Master of the Universe has entered into a 'partnership' with you. Simply put: You matter. Hashem cares about you, wants you, and even 'needs' you in this world. We are entrusted with a Divine purpose, an awesome responsibility to be 'co-creators' in transforming this world into the place it really is, a garden of Divine spiritual delight. Hashem 'depends' on us to carry out the awesome mission of creating a *Dirah b'Tachtonim* / a dwelling place here in the lower, earthly realms for the Essence of Hashem, as it were.

Our Bitachon Atzmi, our ability to trust in our own amazing capabilities, greatness and power is rooted in the trust Hashem has in us, and also in the fact that our souls are חלק אלו-ה ממעל ממש / "truly part of G-d Above" (*Tanya*, 2) — *Shehe-che-zarta Bi Nishmasi* / the soul that *You* have restored in me.

In addition to the custom of reciting the Modeh Ani prayer upon awakening, there is also a visual Kavanah practice that may help a person remember who they truly are — a soul — and to hold onto this awesome and empowering awareness throughout the entire day.

One of the early redactors of the writings of the Arizal and a well-known Bohemian Mekubal, Rav Meir Papirosh (1624-1662), writes in his book *Ohr Yashar* that if a person wants to 'hold on to his soul' when he wakes up in the morning, and remember his name forever, in this world and in the next (*Siddur Shaloh*, Modeh Ani), he should visualize the letters of his name interspersed and interwoven with the letters of the word *Neshamah* / soul. For example, if the person's name is Yaakov, which is spelled Yud-Ayin-Kuf-Beis, the eight letters sequence of Yaakov and Neshamah would become ינעשקמבה / Yud-**Nun**-Ayin-**Shin**-Kuf-**Mem**-Beis-**Hei**. This combination creates a *Yichud* / unity between his name and his Neshamah.

There is a difference in procedure when performing this Yichud on Shabbos. On Shabbos you begin with the Nun of the word Neshamah rather than with the first letter of your own name: in our example, ניעשקמבה.

This is because on Shabbos the reality of your Neshamah, your inner soul, precedes your identity*

On one level, the *Yichud* / unification of the letters of your Hebrew name and the letters of the word *Neshamah* is like a metaphysical combination that opens a lock. It is like a special code that automatically allows your personal identity to connect and unify with your soul, your deeper self, the self of clarity, vision, purpose and connection. Because of this, the mere act of scanning the letters is sufficient to activate it, even without logically understanding the meanings. This practice is called *Habata* / looking, or *Temunah* / 'picturing' or imagining with your mind's eye. There is a positive effect on a person's psyche and inner consciousness by simply scanning the 'image' of the Yichud — by 'dialing the number' as it were, an energetic alignment is created, which sparks the person

* Shabbos is characterized by upper unity and weekdays by lower unity. There are two ways to unify the Name Havayah / Hashem / י-ה-ו-ה with Ado-noi / א-ד-נ-י. The יחודא עילאה / upper unity is symbolized in the unity of these two names beginning with the 'higher' Name of Hashem: **י-א-ה-ד-ו-נ-ה-י**. This represents the prominence of the Higher, and the drawing down of the Higher into the lower, from a place of Unity down into a place of time and space. The realm of Shabbos is of transcendence infusing immanence. There is also a יחודא תתאה / lower unity, which begins with the Aleph of Ado-noi and then the letter Yud of Hashem, and so forth, as in **א-י-ד-ה-נ-ו-י-ה**. This represents the prominence of the lower, as we begin with the Aleph of the lower Name, Ado-noi, and the lower is elevated into the higher. This is the realm of the weekday. When the lower three outer worlds are elevated into the higher world of Atzilus, the lower still remains with the properties of the lower, but it becomes overwhelmed in the presence of the higher. Whereas the Alter Rebbe seems to be *Mechadesh* / innovate and reveal that when there is a full drawing down of the higher (Atzilus) into the lower worlds, as in **י-א-ה-ד-ו-נ-ה-י**, the *Parsa* / division between the two is erased, and the lower becomes one with the higher (perhaps as the ultimate unity of Ayin and Yesh): *Torah Ohr*, Parshas Bo.

to act and react in life in a certain way. On a deeper level, contemplating the meaning of this Yichud arouses the level of *Tevunah* / understanding, in which the conscious mind as well is transformed through the imagery.

What are the mechanics of this Yichud practice? Think for a moment about the sensation you experience when you hear your name called. A definite response is elicited; you react in a particular way. Fascinatingly, people can hear their name above intervening noise. Known as the 'cocktail party syndrome', if you are in a crowded party or airport, for example, and someone mentions your name at a distance, you will hear and register it despite all the other sounds.

Furthermore, when you hear your name called, a certain identity comes up in response. In fact, each variation of your name calls forth a different response. For example, let's say your name is Yaakov. Most people you know may call you Yaakov, but your friends may call you Yanki, and your mother may call you Yankele. If you hear the name 'Yankele', you instinctively think of yourself as a child. If you hear 'Yanki,' you think of yourself as a friend. If you hear 'Yaakov,' your identity as an adult arises; if you hear 'Mister', it suggests some level of distance and formality.

What unifies all these responses is the stimulation of the egoic self, your image of yourself as a physical being born to a certain set of parents, with certain friends, a certain role, job and surroundings. One of the purposes of interweaving your name with the word *Neshamah*, is to create a new identity, so to speak, a new perception of yourself. This 'new name' calls up an identity as a soul within a body, rather than a body that supposedly possesses a soul. Gazing at or scanning your ensouled name is also a way to accustom yourself to identify with your soul's purpose and Divine mission in this world.

Accustoming yourself to seeing yourself as your Yichud can start to give you a new associative response to your normal name. It no longer appears to mean only the son or daughter of so and so, or the person with certain friends or who does this or that work. When someone speaks your name, rather than hearing those references, you can begin to hear a reference to your immortal, true and authentic self, your soul. Your self-image slowly shifts toward your core spiritual identity. You start thinking of yourself as a being created in the Divine image with infinite reservoirs of *Koach* / power, potential and purpose.

Hoda'ah and Bitachon are positive postures relevant during the entire year, but especially during Kislev, the month of miracles. This month makes us aware that our moments of awakening in the morning are crucial and foundational for the entire day; everything depends on our ability to infuse them with Hoda'ah and Bitachon. As soon as we wake up, even before we wash our hands, we can plant seeds of Hoda'ah and Bitachon by making our first definite thought: *Modeh Ani* / I am grateful! Then we can think about who we really are, perhaps using our Yichud, so that we can establish genuine self-confidence in our soul's mission and purpose for the day. In this way, not only do we lay the groundwork to have a truly successful day, we build the *Kelim* / vessels to perceive the miracles of life "in those days, at this time".

Here we learn that one powerful way to develop the *Chush* of sleep, the 'sense' of the month, is precisely by how we wake up in the morning. The Modeh Ani instills in us a firm foundation of Bitachon, which stays with us throughout the day, allowing us to draw upon it in the moments before sleep. This trust allows us to peacefully surrender to the darkness of sleep.

ESSAY 1

'Tractate Chanukah': the Case of the Missing Mesechta

SEVERAL HUNDRED YEARS AFTER THE CHANUKAH EVENT, the great sage Rabbi Yehuda, otherwise known as 'Rebbe', compiled, sorted, edited and published the first accepted documentation of the Oral Tradition of Torah. Before he died in the year 219 CE, he realized the need to preserve the Oral Tradition from the deepening darkness and the impending 'amnesia' of exile. He took the position that "It is a time to act for the sake of Hashem, (therefore we can) 'nullify' Your Torah." This means that for the purpose of preserving the Torah, as exile had begun to take effect and the Jewish People had begun to live dispersed around the globe, Rebbe felt he could bypass the Torah's command to not write down the Oral Torah. For the purpose of the Torah itself, and for the sake of Heaven, sometimes "the nullification of Torah is what actually establishes it" (*Menachos*, 99b). Rebbe therefore published the first widespread, accessible texts representing the Oral Tradition, called *The Mishnah*. Unlike his detailed treatment of Holy Days such as Pesach and even Purim, giving them their own tractates, he did not give a tractate to Chanukah, and scarcely mentioned it elsewhere.

Chanukah is mentioned in the Mishnah only seven times, and only as a marker and aside, and nowhere are its laws and practices explained, for example how we light the candles and when we light them. Later, in the Gemara, Chanukah was described briefly in Maseches Shabbos, after cryptically asking *Mai Chanukah* / "What is Chanukah?" The Zohar, as well, does not even mention Chanukah, despite the rich mysticism of the Yom Tov. Why is there such silence in our foundational writings, and what does it mean about the nature of Chanukah and about our Avodah on these deeply inspiring days?

One of the mentions of Chanukah in the Mishnah deals with bringing the *Bikurim* / first fruits to the Beis haMikdash. The Mishnah says that from Sukkos until Chanukah (which is late for Bikurim, as they should be brought from Shavuos) one can still bring Bikurim, but one does not recite the passages in the Torah relating to Bikurim (*Bikurim*, 1:6). Another mention of Chanukah is with regards to sending out dispatchers to inform the people of the day the new month had been declared in Yerushalayim. At the beginning of Nisan they would be sent out so people could know when Pesach would be, and at the beginning of Kislev to know when Chanukah would be (*Rosh Hashanah*, 1:3). Other mentions are in *Tractate Megilah* with regard to reading the Torah (3:4, 3:6), in *Moed Katan* (3:9) with regard to mourning, and in *Baba Kama* (6:6) with regard to property damage.

Some may argue that Chanukah is not mentioned as a subject in itself because the Yom Tov — the joyous celebration as we know it — developed much later. This argument does not hold up, as the Chanukah mentioned in the Mishnah is in fact described as a Yom Tov on which people light Menorahs. Clearly, they were celebrating the miracles in a festive manner. Let us therefore explore some other possible reasons that discussions of Chanukah are not included in these texts.

MAYBE THERE WAS A TRACTATE CHANUKAH AND IT WAS LOST

There are sources, such as the writings of the Gra of Vilna, that speak of a "lost", small tractate of Gemara called Chanukah, which is one of, or part of, the seven smaller tractates (*Rav Poalim*, Hakdamah. p 8). Today, none of the known "seven small tractates" are about Chanukah, but perhaps there was one and it was lost and replaced by another one. A similar idea is expressed by the Chidah (1724-1806). He writes (*Devarim Achadim*, Drush 32) that in fact, "even today" there *is* a tractate on Chanukah: *Megilas Ta'anis* / the Tractate of Fasts. Keep in mind, that in the times of Chazal, Megilas Ta'anis was a very popular text (מגלת תענית דכתיבא ומנחא *Eiruvin*, 62b). This tractate obviously includes many other subjects, but it does tell us about Chanukah and why we are not allowed to fast during those eight days of celebration.

PERHAPS IT WAS NOT NECESSARY OR DESIRABLE

When Gemara *Shabbos* asks *Mai Chanukah?* / "What is Chanukah..." and briefly describes it, it is quoting from *Megilas Ta'anis*, a text composed before the Mishnah, which speaks about the days on which we are not allowed to fast. One of these days is Chanukah, and there the basic laws of Chanukah are written. For this reason, perhaps it was simply not *necessary* for Rebbe to write a tractate on Chanukah as Megilas Ta'anis was readily available.

Others have wondered that if indeed it is an omission, it might have had to do with the eventual establishment of Jewish sovereignty in the Land of Israel by the Chashmona'im. The Chashmona'im were *Cohanim* / priests from the tribe of Levi who were not meant to rule, and in fact as the Ramban points out their dynasty was fraught with corruption and untimely deaths. The kingship had been promised to the tribe of Yehudah / Judah and not to them. Thus perhaps Rebbe, who was from Yehudah, did not wish to offer the Chashmona'im honor by dedicating an entire tractate to 'their' Holy Day of Chanukah. On the other hand, the Rambam (*Hilchos Chanukah*, 3:1) views the establishment of kingship by the Chashmona'im as a positive development in Jewish history, not a negative event: וגברו בני חשמונאי הכהנים הגדולים והרגום והושיעו ישראל מידם והעמידו מלך מן הכהנים וחזרה מלכות לישראל יתר על מאתים שנה עד החרבן השני / "The Chashmona'im, the high priests, won victories, defeating them (the Syrian Greeks) and saving Israel from their power. They set up a king from among the priests and Israel's kingdom was restored for a period of more than two centuries, until the destruction of the Second Temple." (A good source for the Rambam is the Gemara, *Megilah*, 11a: ולא געלתים בימי יוונים שהעמדתי להם שמעון הצדיק וחשמונאי ובניו ומתתיה כה"ג

לכלותם / "Nor will I abhor them" — this was in the days of the Greeks, when I appointed Shimon haTzaddik for them, and the Chashmona'im and his sons, and Matisyahu the High Priest.") In any case, the answer that Rebbe did not want to write a Tractate Chanukah is troubling: a) While Chanukah did begin with the victory of the Chashmona'im, the miracle of the oil occurred in the Beis haMikdash, and is relevant to everyone, b) Chanukah *is* mentioned in the Mishnah a few times.

It is also plausible that Rebbe does not dedicate a tractate to Chanukah simply because the Yom Tov was so well known. The Rambam (*Pirush haMishnayos*, Menachos, 4:1, haTecheles. See also, Chasam Sofer, on Gitin, 78a) writes that the Mishnah does not speak about the laws of Tefilin, Mezuzah, Tzitzis, because each of these Mitzvos were common knowledge at the times of the Mishnah (כל העניינים התלויין בכל זה מן הדינין ומה שנאמר עליהן בשאלות ותשובות אין ראוי כפי קבלת חבורינו לדבר בהן לפי שאינו אלא מפרש והמשנה לא דברה על אלה המצות דבר מיוחד לכלול דיניהן עד שיהא חייב לפרש אותו וסבת זה בעיני לפי שהיו הדברים האלו מפורסמים בזמן חבור המשנה והיו ענינים ידועים ונהוגים ביד כל העם פרט וכלל ואין ענין מהן נפלא משום אדם וע"כ לא ראה לדבר בהן). The story of Chanukah and the establishment as a Yom Tov was relatively recent to the times of Rebbe — just a few hundred years earlier — so perhaps everyone knew the details of the story and how we celebrate, making it unnecessary to write about it. However, this answer is problematic, because the Mishnah was written as a meta-historical text, relevant for all times, not just for Rebbe's contemporaries.

Moreover, the Mitzvos of Chanukah are different from the Mitzvos of Tefilin and Tzitzis, in that those are performed daily and thus they were familiar to all of Klal Yisrael in the time of Rebbe, just as today. The Mitzvos of Chanukah, on the other hand, while they may have been known during the times of Rebbe, they were only practiced eight days a year, and if they were not written for all generations, they would not be familiar to everyone.

One possible reason is that, because of persecution, the sages would sometimes censor themselves in order to avoid alerting the local powers of certain information. Imagine the reaction in Rome if they had heard that the Jewish people are celebrating their revolt. Also, publicizing the celebration could have inspired other peoples, and even other Jews, to revolt, which the rabbis did not want at this time, following the disastrous uprising after the destruction of the Second Beis HaMikdash.

Being that Rebbe was in a position of power and in close friendship with the local Roman ruler, perhaps he would not wish to elaborate on relatively recent events that could appear as a glorification of rebellion or even a call to take up arms against the local Romans. Writing down the story of Chanukah and the ways of celebrating it could seem like the publicization of a new Holy Day of aspirations for political autonomy, logically associated with a desire for freedom from colonial Roman rule.

There are problems with this concept of self-censorship as well: a) if the issue was that the history was too recent, the story of Purim was also relatively recent to the times of the Mishnah, and yet, there is a *Tractate Megilah*, dealing with the laws and practices of Purim; b) Chanukah celebrates our victory of the Greeks (Assyrians) and the Romans themselves had conquered Greece some 350 years before the Mishnah was written. Censoring the celebration of Chanukah would therefore not have been needed.

WAS CHANUKAH ANNULLED?

There is a very interesting passage in Gemara (*Rosh Hashanah*, 18b) amid a debate on the status of *Megilas Ta'anis* following the destruction of the Second Beis haMikdash. *Megilas Ta'anis* mentions days of celebration on which one was not allowed to fast. Some sages say that when the Beis haMikdash was standing, in a time of peace, the celebratory days in *Megilas Ta'anis* were upheld, but once the Beis haMikdash was destroyed, "*Megilas Ta'anis* was annulled," and the celebratory days were no longer to be upheld. Others argue that "*Megilas Ta'anis* was not annulled," and the celebratory days still apply today.

So, the question is, if the source for Chanukah is *Megilas Ta'anis*, then according to the opinions that "*Megilas Ta'anis* is annulled," why do we celebrate Chanukah?

In fact, the Gemara brings down a story in which a public fast was established on a day of Chanukah in the city of Lud — consistent with the opinion that "*Megilas Ta'anis* was annulled" along with the Yom Tov of Chanukah. However, the Gemara continues, that the sages, Rebbe Eliezer and Rebbe Yehoshua went to Lud during that fast day. Rebbe Eliezer bathed and Rebbe Yehoshua took a haircut, showing that the fast had no validity, and they declared, "Go and fast (to atone) for the fact that you fasted (on Chanukah)!"

The final answer in the Gemara is that we still celebrate Chanukah because the miracle is public knowledge. Rashi writes, כבר הוא גלוי לכל ישראל ע"י שנהגו בו המצות והחזיקו בו כשל תורה ולא נכון לבטלו / "All of Israel know of this holiday and observe its practices like the laws in the actual Torah, and so it is not correct to annul it."

From all the above, it is clear that after the destruction of the Beis haMikdash, at least until the time of Rebbe Eliezer and Rebbe Yehoshua, the status of Chanukah was uncertain, and some people actually followed the ruling that it was annulled, and did not celebrate Chanukah. This implies that at some point after the destruction of the Beis haMikdash, Chanukah was reestablished as a Yom Tov. (This is also related to the reason why we celebrate Chanukah. If it is basically the commemoration of a military victory, as the Book of Chashmona'im states, then once we were no longer in Israel and under our own rule, it would make no sense to celebrate it anymore. But, if Chanukah is about the miracle of the oil, the resting of the Shechinah upon and within the world, and the revelation of the Oral Torah, etc, then it makes sense to continue to celebrate it). And before that point, Rebbe may have made a decision to not include Chanukah as a tractate, if a) he agreed with the opinion that "it was annulled", or if b) he did not wish to rule either for or against the reestablishment of the Holy Day.

These answers are also problematic, as Rebbe compiled the Mishnah some 130 years after the destruction of the Beis haMikdash. Surely by that time a consensus would have been reached to reestablish Chanukah, especially after the story with Rebbe Eliezer and Rebbe Yehoshua had taken place. And again, Rebbe does mention Chanukah a few times in the Mishnah, so it must have been a universally accepted Yom Tov in his time (as indicated by the above Gemara and Rashi).

We have searched extensively, but we are still left with the mystery of the lack of teachings in our foundational texts on Chanukah. To find a satisfying answer we will need to look more deeply.

REFLECTED LIGHT

Perhaps the omission of details in the Mishnah is hiding in plain sight: it is intimately related to the actual celebration and theme of Chanukah itself. This could be the same reason that the Yom Tov of Chanukah is not mentioned in the Zohar (See *Tiferes Tzvi*, 3:397, 465). Being that Chanukah is so deeply related to the development and transmission of the Oral Torah, we should consider that Rebbe purposely chose to keep the laws and principles of Chanukah oral and not write them down. Even though he had taken upon himself to write down the foundations of the Oral Torah, he realized that it would become somewhat 'fixed' upon being written, and Rebbe wished to keep Chanukah purely oral, unfixed, fluid, vibrant and expressed within the higher intuition of the People.

The oral aspect of Torah is a manifestation of the *Ohr Chozer* / Reflected Light, a light that emerges from darkness, an answer that comes about through question and debate. Questions correspond to the darkness of exile, and answers and clarity correspond to the light of Redemption. The hope and glimmer of light that emerges from within darkness, the Oral Tradition, is rooted in human intellect and the holy intuition of the sages, as distinct from the prophets who received the *Ohr Yashar* / Direct Light, the more 'fixed' light of revelation from Above.

A prophet, as defined in the era of the First Beis haMikdash, is one who quiets and empties his or her mind to receive transmission from Above, and a definitive instruction is relayed to them to transmit to Klal Yisrael. As the Second Beis haMikdash period began, prophecy came to a close and the era of the sages began. A sage is one who grapples with their intellect, and through Ohr Chozer, grasps sparks and hints of the light of revelation as it manifests 'below'. This is the specialty of Chanukah, the only universal Yom Tov that is purely from the sages — not mentioned in the revealed Written Torah at all, rather existing within the Oral Torah alone.*

In this way, the reason that Chanukah is not elaborated in the Mishnah is consistent with the overall understanding of the theme of Chanukah itself, the emergence of the Reflected Light and the drawing down of the Divine Presence through our own actions and initiative. This is also the nature of the Second Beis haMikdash period versus the First Beis haMikdash period. The era of the first Beis haMikdash is the age of the prophets and Tanach — "revelation from Above". The era of the Second Beis haMikdash is the time of the sages, the revealing of Torah she-b'al-Peh, — "revelation from Below".

By keeping the details of the way we celebrate Chanukah, and being aware of why we celebrate it, we are safekeeping the Oral Tradition and aligning ourselves with the Ohr Chozer and the consciousness of the sages and illumined teachers down to the present day. We are strengthening the light that shines in the darkness, the Divine Presence that travels with us in exile and resides deep within the recesses of the human mind.

---

* Purim was established by sages, without prophetic revelations from Above, but *Megilas Ester* was accepted into Tanach, so it became part of Torah she-b'Kesav. The customs of Simchas Torah were intuitively created by the later sages, but the day of Simchas Torah is really the second day of Shemini Atzeres in the Diaspora, and in Eretz Yisrael it is in fact celebrated on Shemini Atzeres.

Not only is the 'way' we light, the Halachah of the Mitzvah, an expression of the living Oral Tradition of Torah, but, it could be argued, the fact that we light at all is an expression of the Oral Tradition. In fact, it is possible that the laws were not written down because originally they only recited Hallel and Hoda'ah on Chanukah, as the Gemara says, לשנה אחרת קבעום ועשאום ימים טובים בהלל והודאה / "The following year they established and enacted Yamim Tovim with Hallel and Hoda'ah." Nothing is recorded here about lighting candles. Of course, at that time the Beis haMikdash was standing, and so the sacred Menorah was being lit there, so what would be the point of each person lighting in their home? Clearly, it is possible that they did not light personal Menorahs until after the Churban / destruction. The inner reason why Rebbe, intentionally or unintentionally — in any case, 'prophetically' — did not delineate the laws of Chanukah in the Mishnah, was so that it could remain a living expression of Torah. In fact, some of the most dominant images of Chanukah, certainly for children, are the Dreidel and Chanukah Gelt and gifts, and these are relatively new *Minhagim* / customs, part of the living expression of Torah. Chanukah is a living Yom Tov that resides deep within the hearts and minds of Klal Yisrael, and thus over time different Minhagim developed, vibrantly elaborating on its inner significance.

A HIDDEN UTTERANCE

It is brought down in the name of the Baal Shem Tov and his students, that the spiritual work done in the *Mishkan* / travelling 'Temple' corresponds to the *Ma'asei B'reishis* / Divine Acts of Creation, the Ten Utterances of "Let there be...," and the work of the Menorah, its lighting, is connected to the First Utterance, the word

Bereishis. (There are nine utterances of "Let there be...." The tenth is therefore a 'hidden' utterance: the word *Bereshis* itself: *Rosh Hashanah*, 32a. Maharsha, ad loc. Although see *Zohar* 3, 11b and *Pirkei d'Rebbe Eliezer*, 1.) This *Ma'amar Sasum* / Hidden Utterance corresponds to the Ein Sof — or as the Zohar sees it, the *Ayin* / Divine Nothingness, an ineffable dimension higher than Chochmah. This is the level of Keser / Crown, soaring above all of the *Midos* / attributes and Acts of Creation.

As the Menorah is connected to the Hidden Utterance, in which there are no actual words spoken (it does not say, '*Hashem said, Bereishis...*'), Moshe had trouble understanding how to make the Menorah. As an expression of the hidden transcendent light of Keser, it could not be committed to the world of words and outward expression. The Light of the Menorah, too, is an indicator of Keser; a flame leaps upward, pointing toward a higher realm, the unutterable reality of Keser. Chanukah could not be delineated and described by writing, as it belongs to a reality beyond words, percolating within the deepest recesses of Klal Yisrael's consciousness and imagination.

HIDDEN WITHIN THE PEOPLE

Chanukah evolved over time, with the fluid and unfolding Oral Tradition. When Klal Yisrael accepted upon themselves to light a Menorah, it came from their deepest spiritual instincts — not from instructions in a book. Perhaps the strongest example of this process is the Minhag, which is not even mentioned by our sages in the Gemara, to light the Menorah on Chanukah in a *Shul* / synagogue, and do so with a *Berachah* / blessing.* Reciting a Berachah is a stringent matter; we are careful to recite a blessing with Hashem's Name only when it is clearly warranted by Halachah. How can we recite a Berachah on a 'mere' Minhag? The fact that we do, demonstrates the way that *Minhag Yisrael* / a universal custom of the People of Israel 'becomes' *Din* / Divine Law; it is incorporated within the Oral Tradition and in this way becomes part of the way Torah is practiced.

Rebbe Yehudah, the master and guardian of the Oral Law, recognized this power of the People to access Divine Wisdom within. He refrained from codifying and writing the details of Chanukah in *The Mishnah* because he wanted to allow the traditions of Chanukah to continue to flow fresh from the depths of intuitive wisdom of the sages of Klal Yisrael.

Just as the Ohr haGanuz is not 'missing' but rather hidden within the Torah and within us in our encounter with Torah, Tractate Chanukah is not 'missing', it is hidden — within us.

---

* *Shulchan Aruch,* Orach Chayim 671:7, this is based on the opinion of many Rishonim: see Beis Yoseph, *Orach Chayim*, 671: וז"ל הריב"ש בתשובה המנהג הזה להדליק בב"ה מנהג ותיקין היא משום פירסומי ניסא כיון שאין אנו יכולין לקיים המצוה כתקנה להדליק כל א' בפתח ביתו מבחוץ מפני שיד העו"ג תקיפה ומברכין ע"ז כמו שמברכין על הלל דר"ח אע"פ שאינו אלא מנהג. Others argue that a blessing should not be recited: *Shu't Chacham Tzvi*, 88. *Maharam Schick, Yoreh De'ah*, 347. There is also a custom to recite Half Hallel on Rosh Chodesh, and there is a big debate among the Rishonim if a blessing should be recited. For example, the Rambam and Rashi hold that no blessing should be recited. The Rif (*Shabbos*, 24b), Rabbeinu Tam (Tosefos, *Ta'anis*, 28b. Tosefos, *Erechin*, 10b), the Tur in the name of the Rosh (Tur, *Orach Chayim*, 422), and the Ran, however, maintain that we do make blessings over such important customs: see *Shulchan Aruch*, Orach Chayim, 422:2.

ESSAY 2

The World as it Appears vs The World as it Reveals

According to the Hellenist worldview, 'seeing' is believing; only objectivity is of value. The body and the empirical were worshipped and the mind was viewed as the apex of human potential and nobility. For this reason, even during the persecution in the Chanukah narrative, the Greeks allowed the Jewish People to study the Torah and appreciate its beauty, so long that it was purely an intellectual, non-spiritual pursuit.

להשכיחם תורתך / "...to make them forget Your Torah" — this was the aim of the Greeks. Again, the actual study did not disturb the Greeks' worldview. To the contrary, the Greeks were lovers of wisdom and relished intellectual argumentation and dialogue. In fact, the Greeks were the first to commission the translation of the Torah (*Megilah*, 9a). Rather, what troubled the Greeks was the study of Torah as "Your" Torah, as a connection to the Divine. And more deeply, and perhaps paradoxically, the Greeks waged battle specifically against Torah she-b'al Peh. They despised and fought against the elaboration, the 'subjective' experience and interpretation of the Divine Presence that was alive and circulating throughout Klal Yisrael.

Torah she-b'al-Peh / the Oral Torah or rabbinic tradition is the 'subjective' interpretation and truth of Torah inspired by and aligned with the objective truth of *Torah she-b'Ksav* / the Written Torah, or Tanach. The living wisdom of Torah she-b'al-Peh pulsates in our hearts, in both personal and communal experience, and is deeply rooted in the collective imagination of Klal Yisrael.

Before any attempt to put it into writing, this continuously expanding stream of understanding and guidance was transmitted from teacher to student and parent to child. Its living lineage began with Moshe, when he descended from Mount Sinai on Yom Kippur conveying forgiveness for the Sin of the Golden Calf. Moshe transmitted it to Yehoshua, and Yehoshua to the Elders, and the transmission continues in each generation until it reaches us. The idea of a living, subjective, Oral Tradition of Torah was anathema to the Greeks, and they sought to eliminate its teaching and practice.

In their extreme arrogance, the Greeks commanded Klal Yisrael, כתבו על קרן השור שאין לכם חלק באלהי ישראל, "Write on the horn of a bull, that you have no *Cheilek* / part in the G-d of Israel" (*Medrash*

Rabbah, Bereishis, 2:4). Why the "horn of a bull"? Perhaps the Greeks were suggesting to Klal Yisrael, 'You have built a Golden Calf, a "bull", so you no longer have a Cheilek in the G-d of Israel,' Chas veShalom.

From another perspective, a horn is an outgrowth of the head. When a horn is connected to the bull's head, it can be understood as a *Mashal* / analogy of Torah she-b'al-Peh, a living outgrowth connected to its 'head' or source, the Torah she-b'Ksav. This is why the Greeks were demanding that we write on a horn that was no longer a "part" of its head; they were attempting to discredit the Torah she-b'al-Peh by claiming that it no longer has a connection to Torah she-b'Ksav.'

It seems the Greeks were arguing, 'Yes, there is a Transcendent G-d, there is an objectively true Written Torah, and G-d talks to humanity and reveals wisdom to us. It is just that due to your sin you can never again have a "part" in Him and partner with Him in the unfolding process of Torah.' This is an attack against the Torah she-b'al-Peh, the Torah of holy subjectivity within the heart of Klal Yisrael. It asserts that "you", the subject, no longer have a living, vibrant and current connection to the Divine "You", HaKadosh Baruch Hu. You are cut off as a people. Only the objective Written Torah is valid, and your subjective Torah she-b'al-Peh is, like you, a dead, detached 'horn'.

Furthermore, they claimed, 'You have no connection to the G-d *of Israel;* you have forfeited a private, subjective, 'national' relationship with G-d; only the universal, objective G-d, as it were, is now valid. The words "of Israel" allude to the unique connection and collaborative partnership with HaKadosh Baruch Hu that constitutes Torah she-b'al-Peh, which is precisely what the Greeks sought to eradicate. They denied the truth that HaKadosh Baruch Hu is at once universal *and* in a unique love relationship with Klal Yisrael; at once the Master of the Universe *and* the G-d of Israel.

This Hellenist worldview began to threaten the deeper purpose and mission of Klal Yisrael, as it appealed to a large number of oppressed and assimilated Jews of the time, drawing them away from the oral tradition. This worldview is a *Kelipah* / parasitical shell encasing the real light of objectivity. While it fed off the holy light of the Written Torah, Hellenism intended to cut off any subjective spiritual experience of it — and ultimately to cut off the Jewish People from the Indwelling Divine Presence. The spiritual victory of Chanukah is the victory of Toras she-b'al-Peh over the intellectual Kelipah of the Yevanim.

The Greeks were philosophers, and their Kelipa represents the *Achorayim* / 'other side' or dark side of Torah she-b'al-Peh. The fundamental difference (*Le'Havdil* / to separate between the sacred and mundane) between the *Chidushim* / innovations of Chazal and Greek Philosophy, is Chazal's understanding that while the human intellect is a powerful tool, Torah she-b'al-Peh is rooted in Transcendent Wisdom, not in human intellect. In fact, the principles of all Chidushim that were ever innovated by wise students of the Torah were originally *Nitna miSinai* / given by HaKadosh Baruch Hu to Moshe at Mount Sinai (*Yerushalmi*, *Pe'ah*, 2:4. *Megilah*, 19b. *Menachos*, 29b). This is how the Transcendent, objective truth is revealed within the microcosmic, particular, subjective truth.

POWER OF THE MENORAH

As the *Galus* / exile of the Greeks is connected to intellectualism with no sense of a higher, transcendent level of consciousness, the Chanukah miracle occurs specifically with the oil and the Menorah, as the Menorah corresponds to the Torah (*Yalkut Reuveini*, Terumah). In fact, it can be understood as a structure that joined and united the Torah she-b'Kesav and the Torah she-b'al-Peh. Although the objective commandment to make a Menorah is given in the Written Torah, Moshe was not able to 'picture' how it would be made (*Menachos*, 29a); in other words, the commandment required interpretation to be performed. There was a mystery beyond its immediate image, and he needed an 'explanation', so-to-speak, alluding to the idea of Torah she-b'al-Peh.

The following is how the structure of the Menorah itself is actually an image of the Written Torah:

• The seven branches of the Menorah correspond to the seven words of the first *Pasuk* / verse in *Bereishis*, the first of the Five Books of the Torah.

• The eleven *Kaftorim* / almond bud designs of the Menorah, correspond to the eleven words in the first Pasuk of Shemos, the second book of the Torah.

• The nine flowers of the Menorah, correspond to the nine words of the first Pasuk in Vayikra, the third book of the Torah.

• While the Menorah is described as having a height of eighteen *Tefachim* / handbreadths, it was actually seventeen full Tefachim plus part of a Tefach. These seventeen full Tefachim correspond to the seventeen words of the first Pasuk in *Bamidbar*, the fourth book of the Torah

• The twenty-two cup-shaped designs correspond to the twenty-two words of the first Pasuk in *Devarim*, the fifth book of the Torah.

More than a battle against Torah *she-b'Ksav* / the Written Torah, the world of pure transcendence, the Greek Galus represents a spiritual battle against Torah she-b'al-Peh, which is the unity between transcendence and immanence, between the world of utter objectivity and the inner world of subjectivity. As such, the symbol of Chanukah, the Menorah, reflects and represents the Torah she-b'al-Peh. This can be seen in the seven branches of the Menorah, representing the seven general branches of human wisdom, as cited by many Rishonim: grammar, rhetoric, logic, arithmetic, music, geometry and astronomy.

The pure oil that rests above each branch and is lit, illuminating the darkness, represents the Torah wisdom revealed through the minds of the sages, which rises upward through the flickering flames of our *Avodah* / spiritual service, connecting us to the Transcendent One, Above. Thus, today we kindle a Menorah with eight branches, to allude to the dimension of eight, transcendence, and the 'eternality' of the Torah she-b'al-Peh. The adornment of upside down cups on the branches and base of the Menorah enact the downward emanation of light, the idea of the *Mekabel* / receiver of Torah, and especially that of Torah she-b'al-Peh. The buds and blossoms are also an allusion to Torah she-ba'al-Peh. Appropriately, Rav Tarfon used to exclaim, when he heard a skillful and reasonable *Chidush* / innovative Torah thought, *Kaftor uPerach* / buds and blossoms! (*Medrash Rabbah*, Bereishis, 91:9).

During the Second Temple period, when there was an abundance of Torah she-b'al-Peh, the Menorah proved its strength and the miracle of Chanukah occurred (See Netziv, *Emek Davar*, Parshas Tetzaveh, 27:20).

SUBJECTIVE TORAH

Every Yom Tov besides Chanukah is established around a miracle or event that was objectively experienced by the entire Klal Yisrael. For example, *Yetzias Mitzrayim* / the Going Out of Egypt, Matan Torah, and even Purim, were experienced firsthand by all of Klal Yisrael — millions of people. The miracle of the oil (assuming the Menorah that the Chashmona'im used was at the time stationed within the Beis haMikdash and not in the courtyard) was experienced by only a select few. Only the Cohanim (and the Chasmona'im were Cohanim) who were able to enter within the *Kodesh* / Holy area, could see the Menorah and observe the miracle of the oil. In this way, the miracle was 'visually' experienced by only a few people, and it was later described orally to the Klal. When the Klal heard about the miracle of the oil, their *Emunah* / faith was aroused, the message resonated within their hearts, and the miracle became real to them as if they had seen it.

When an event happens in front of a multitude, it is confirmed by the collective and thus established as an objective truth. Any subjectivity within the experience is outshone by the objectivity of its experience. For example, if one individual at Mount Sinai somehow had doubts whether or not he had perceived the lightning at Matan Torah, inevitably, his private experience would have been corrected and more acutely subsumed into the objective experienced truth of the Klal, in which "*All* the People saw the thunder and the lightning" (*Shemos*, 20:18). Chanukah, by contrast, occurred in isolation from the Klal, in the privacy of the Beis haMikdash. It was not experienced in an atmosphere of objective 'seeing', nor was it confirmed by the people directly. This is arguably the first real 'collective' revelation of Torah she-b'al-Peh.*

* Regarding the kingdom of the Chashmona'im, the Ramban writes (*Bereishis*, 49:10) that since לא־יסור שבט מיהודה / "The scepter (of kingship) shall not depart from (the tribe of) Yehudah," the Chashmona'im were punished for anointing themselves as kings, as they were from the tribe of Levi, not Yehudah. וזה היה עונש החשמונאים, שמלכו בבית שני, כי היו חסידי עליון ואלמלא הם נשתכחו התורה והמצות מישראל, ואף על פי כן נענשו עונש גדול, כי ארבעת בני חשמונאי הזקן החסידים המולכים זה אחר זה, עם כל גבורתם והצלחתם, נפלו ביד אויביהם בחרב / "And this was (the cause for) the punishment of the Chashmona'im who reigned during (the time) of the Second Temple, as they were (otherwise) lofty pious ones, and were it not for them, the Torah and the commandments would have been forgotten from Israel. Nonetheless, they were punished with a great punishment: four of the sons of the elder Chashmona'im who reigned one after the other, (in spite) all of their strength and their success, fell to the hands of their enemies by the sword." They were punished to the extent that, as the Gemara says, "Whoever says he is a descendant from the house of the Chashmona'im, know that he is a slave" (*Kidushin*, 70b). This is because Hurdas killed the entire House of Chashmona'im (*Baba Basra*, 3b), and he himself was a 'slave' in the Kingdom of the Chashmona'im. Yet, according to the Rambam, it seems that the establishment of the kingdom of Chashmona'im is a positive development. These are the words of the Rambam: עד שרחם עליהם אלהי אבותינו והושיעם מידם והצילם וגברו בני חשמונאי הכהנים הגדולים והרגום והושיעו ישראל מידם והעמידו מלך מן הכהנים וחזרה מלכות לישראל יתר על מאתים שנה עד החרבן השני / (During the period of the second Temple, when the Greek kings were in power, they proclaimed decrees against the Jewish people…the people of Israel were sorely distressed by their enemies, who oppressed them ruthlessly) "until the G-d of our fathers took pity, saved and rescued them from the hands of the tyrants. The Chashmona'im

great priests won victories, defeating them and saving Israel from their power. They set up a king from among the priests and Israel's kingdom was restored for a period of more than two centuries, until the destruction of the Second Temple" (*Hilchos Chanukah*, 3:1).

These opinions seem diametrically opposite each other, which in itself is not an issue, but what would the Rambam do with the clear injunction, לא־יסור שבט מיהודה / "the leadership and loyalty belong to the tribe of Yehudah," not Levi? The Chashmona'im were *Cohanim* / priests, from the tribe of Levi.

Regarding the Gemara that says that all the descendants from the house of the Chashmona'im were killed, Reb Tzadok of Lublin (*Resisei Layla*, Os 57) comments that it does not literally mean every single person from the House of Chashmona'im was killed, rather that Hurdas killed all the 'known' children from the House of Chashmona'im, but some others, those whose *Yichus* / ancestry was not *b'Pirsum* / publicized, but rather was hidden, were not killed: אבל ברור בעיני דהכונה שלא נשתייר מזרעו **בפירסום** ומי שיתייחס אחריו וקטלינהו לכולהי מרותיה היינו כל אותם שמצא והם נענשו בעונם והשאר נחבאו והעלימו עצמם **ולא פירסמו** יחוסם

While Reb Tzadok means this quite literally, perhaps he is also suggesting a type of 'hidden lineage' that connects the kingdom and dynasty of the Chashmona'im to the tribe of Yehudah.

Cohanim are all descendants of Aharon / Aaron, and perhaps, as Reb Tzadok writes elsewhere, since Aaron was married to a woman from the House of Yehudah, Elisheva, the sister of Nachshon ben Aminadov from their collective mother's side, the Cohanim are indeed from the Tribe of Yehudah (although, Halachically tribal lineage follows only the patrilineal line). In this way, a Cohen is a descendant in the 'revealed' sense on the father's side (the masculine being the 'revealed' dimension, physiologically and thus spiritually), and from Aaron. Yet, the 'hidden' ancestry of a Cohen, that is, from his mother's side (the feminine being a more hidden, inward dimension, physiologically and thus spiritually), they are actually from the house of Yehudah. This is the 'non-Pirsum' Yichus of every Cohen, and the Chashmona'im all had this ancestry. Those who were killed had revealed their Yichus to Aaron HaCohen. Those who remained alive, who were not "punished", were those who did not reveal their Yichus, meaning that they literally and metaphorically were connected to their Yichus from their mother's side. The Chashmona'im connected to the mantle of *Malchus* / kingship through their 'matriarch', who was from Yehudah. As explored throughout the text, Chanukah is intricately bound with Torah she-b'al Peh. In this way, the Chashmona'im, who linked themselves to their past via their maternal ancestor, did so as well because they, and the time

What is more, if, theoretically, the 'subjective' miracles of Chanukah would have been written down by the prophets as part of the *Kesuvim* / Writings of the Torah she-b'Kesav, Chanukah would have entered the realm of 'objective truth', as it were. But the miracles of Chanukah, by nature, belong to the realm of 'subjective' or 'individual' truth, even while being universally recognized and accepted. This is the *Chidush* / novelty or unique reality of Chanukah, and the source of its power. This is, perhaps, why Rebbe did not write a 'Tractate Chanukah', and why it does not appear as a full subject in the Zohar. It needed to stay oral, and continue to be part of a dynamic conversation between people, and a living, vibrant Torah.

Greek wisdom is centered around empirical knowledge — only what you can 'see' is true and worth probing. There is an 'image' and nothing behind it, no unseen world of mystery or subjectivity. The Greek philosophers argued that 'seeing is believing'.

---

period, was specifically connected to the quality of 'mother' which is Torah she-b'al-Peh. Upon the verse that says אל תטוש תורת אמך / do not forsake the Torah of your Mother [*Mishlei*, 1:8], the Zohar teaches us that this refers to Torah she-b'al-Peh. As the Alter Rebbe explains in the name of the Zohar [*Tanya*, Igeres HaKodesh, 29. See also, *Maor Einayim*, Emor 3], the Written Torah is similar to the father, who inseminates and gives the raw idea, yet it is only in the womb of the mother where the fetus becomes articulated and fully developed. Similarly, the written Torah instructs us on the general idea of the Mitzvah, as for example to tie a sign upon our arms, and the oral aspect of Torah reveals the details of the Mitzvah, for example, black, square boxes with scrolls written therein, i.e.; Tefillin. Simply this means, that תורת אמך / the Torah of the mother is תורה שבעל פה. And this is why, in the times of the second Beis haMikdash, when there began the revealing and articulation of Torah she-b'al-Peh, the Kings of Israel were connected to the line of Yehudah from their 'mother's side'.

In other words, what you see with the naked eye is what is most real. The eye perceives physical things, therefore physicality is of utmost importance. As such, the ancient Greeks (and for that matter, most of modern Western Civilization) worshipped only what can be seen, such as nature, art, sports, sculpture, architecture and theatre. Even today, within our every-day, modern English, founded on Latin and Greek, an idea is called an 'in-sight'. We say things like, 'I see what you are saying,' to express our comprehension. The word 'idea' itself comes from a Latin root related to the word 'video'. All of these metaphors emphasize the act of seeing. *Le'havdil* / to separate between mundane and the sacred topics, Torah Wisdom is centered around the fact that what you 'see' is merely a facade, and deeper seeing allows you to 'hear' what is beyond the image of physicality.

What is present in the immediate vicinity is what can be observed with the eye, but we can hear what is off in the distance, both literally and metaphorically. Hearing opens us to the world beyond the immediate and tangible, the world of Transcendence. For this reason, Torah she-b'al-Peh begins to flower during the reign of Alexander the Great, and in the times of Shimon HaTzadik, as the name Shimon comes from the root-word meaning to 'hear'. During the revelation of the Written Torah, Klal Yisrael "saw the sounds" at Sinai, in the conversational and interpretive process of revealing Oral Torah, however, we must listen deeply to "hear the images", so to speak, to ascertain their deeper meaning, and implicit significance. (This is the level of Binah within Chochmah. Additionally, the people "heard" about the miracle that occurred in the Beis HaMikdash).*

---

*On the Pasuk אשר אין בה מום, says the *Zohar* (2, 237), דא מלכות יוון דאינון קריבין לארח מהימנותא / "This refers to the Greek kingdom, which is *close* to the path

Seeing is immediate and self-evident; there is usually little or no need for processing or for subjective interpretation. (Although even in seeing there is no real objectivity, as we see through the prism of our consciousness. We do not see things the way they are, rather the way *we* are). What you see is what you get; the image, or the 'means', is, in this sense, its own 'end'. There is nothing beyond what you see, if you choose to just see.

The world of the observable image is the world of the Greeks. As such, Greek thought and worship, idolized the 'means' of perception as 'ends' in themselves; meaning that an image is just that, nothing more, expressing no deeper significance other than its appearance on the surface. Interestingly, the Greeks were sports enthusiasts, and perhaps even invented what we call today sports — the idea of challenge for the sake of challenge, not for any utility,

---

of true faith." Regarding this, Rikanti writes (Parshas Chukos, 2), אמר על הפלוסופים קדומים הנוטה בקצת דבריהם לדברי רבותינו ז"ל / "This refers to the early philosophers whose words tend to resemble slightly the words of our Rabbis." And "early philosophers" refers to the pre-Aristotelian philosophers: Rav Yoseph Ergos, *Shomer Emunim haKadmon*, 1:37. Rav Menasha ben Yisrael, *Nishmas Chayim,* 4: 21. A difference between Plato and Aristotle is that the highest sense according to Plato is the sense of hearing, while according to Aristotle, the highest sense is the sense of sight: Rav Yehudah Abarbanel, *Vikuach Al Ahavah*, p. 41-42. Interestingly, the seeing vs. hearing debate is also an argument between the *Mekubalim* and the *Chokrim* / Philosophers. The Chokrim, the Even Ezra (*Shemos* 3:6, 20:1), the Ralbag and others, argue for the supremacy of 'sight'. See *Reishis Chochmah*, Sha'ar haYirah, 8. The Maharal, *Derech haChayim*, 2:9. *Sefer haBris,* 1, Ma'amar 17:5. Whereas the Mekubalim (the Ramban, *Emunah uBitachon*, 18, Rabbeinu Yonah, *Sha'arei Teshuvah*, Sha'ar 2:12, Rabbeinu Bachya, *Kad Kemach,* Zenus Halev v'Ha'ayin, 7, Shemos, 3:7. Rikanti, *Bereishis*, 29:32, Rav Yoseph Yavetz, *Pirush Avos,* 6:2, and many others) argue that 'hearing' is the highest and deepest sense.

benefit or even higher self-development. They espoused art for art's sake — not for any redemptive value, nor for any revelation of the mystery of life. They sought physical pleasure for pleasure's sake, unrelated to true love or procreation. For them, life did not have a larger or deeper purpose, and history did not have a trajectory or goal. Torah values and spirituality were intolerable to them, representing everything they denied.

In stark contrast to worshiping observable phenomena, means as ends in themselves, the Torah teaches us to look deeper and recognize that physical reality is in fact a means to an ultimately deeper end goal. On one level, the entire Torah can be understood as teaching us that everything, all of life, reality and history, has a deeper meaning, and all of life and the entire world are but means to a brighter, more meaningful, holier end. One eats not merely for pleasure, but so one will have strength to learn Torah and do acts of Chesed. One has intimacy in order to have children and nurture love and connectivity. History is moving toward Redemption; *Olam haZeh* / this world is moving towards *Olam haBa* / the World to Come.

This is yet another deeper reason that the celebration of Chanukah is activated by lighting an actual flame, a truly primordial, elemental image. Imagery, as explained, is part of the world of the Greeks, the world of the immediately perceivable, where there is no ultimate purpose or 'end', for every means is its own end. On Chanukah we celebrate the victory over darkness and the opaque vision of materialistic imagery, by harnessing a visual image that silently screams *transcendence*. The nature of a flame is to leap upwards, reaching higher than itself, grasping at and pointing to what is 'beyond' itself. The image of a flame is 'imageless', as it were: it constantly fades in and out of existence, and as it leaps upwards it indicates and reveals its (and our) connection to that which is above and beyond images.

This too is the nature of the Oral Torah, in which Divine Transcendent Wisdom becomes revealed and articulated through the properties of the human mind. As the mind grasps the truths of the Oral Torah, it recognizes that these 'innovations' too were given by HaKadosh Baruch Hu at Sinai. In this recognition, the mind submits to that which is beyond the mind. Our Sages tell us: כל מה שתלמיד ותיק עתיד לחדש ניתן למשה בסיני / "Every *Chidush* / every authentic innovation in Torah that is revealed by a dedicated student, was given to Moshe at Mount Sinai (Yerushalmi, *Peah*, 2:4. *Medrash Rabbah*, Koheles, 1:9, 2). This teaching seems paradoxical; if it is an innovation, how was it 'given on Mount Sinai'? And if the insight was originally given on Mount Sinai, how is it a Chidush? The answer is that the Chidush comes not *from* us, rather *through* us, and its core is forever rooted in the original revelation at Sinai, beyond the mind. Whenever we light our Menorah, whenever we 'hear' or study and practice the Oral Tradition, we are participating in this miraculous spiritual 'victory' of the hidden objective truth that shines within the revealed darkness of subjective knowledge. Like a flame, the Oral Torah is forever connected to the wisdom beyond human knowledge and imagery.

On an even deeper level, in contrast to the Greek paradigm of life, the Torah teaches us that not only are all of our activities and all of life a 'means towards an end,' but, 'the end *is in* the means itself.' In this gordian knot is a total transformation of the Greek idea that there is no real end, and thus it is that the means is to be considered the end in itself. Truly, life *is* a means towards an end, and ultimately, that end is within this means. This suggests a profound way of living in which, for example, eating itself can be a Mitzvah and a tangible way to know Hashem, and intimacy itself, not just its metaphor, can be a sacred experience of Yichud, unity. This is the complete *transformation* of the Greek *Kelipah* / negativity and *Galus* / exile, and it is the deeper power and intention of lighting our Chanukah Menorahs; the light shines, and yet the oil remains.

Lighting the Menorah on Chanukah is thus not a means to an end, rather its purpose, its end, is in the means itself. Lighting Shabbos or Yom Tov candles is performed for the *Kavod* / honor of Shabbos and so that we can enjoy the *Oneg* / pleasure of eating our food in a well-lit room. The kindling of Shabbos and Yom Tov candles brings joy, honor and pleasure into the home; that is their utility, so to speak. The lights of Chanukah, by contrast, are not for any utilitarian purpose, in fact, "we do not have permission to use them, only to see them," as we say in the prayers recited after we kindle the Menorah. The lighting is for the purpose of lighting itself. This is why הדלקה עושה מצוה / *Hadlakah Oseh Mitzvah* / the Mitzvah is accomplished by the very act of lighting the Menorah, not by the fact that the lights remain lit afterwards, whereas on Shabbos or Yom Tov a major part of the Mitzvah is that the candle should remain lit (therefore, מות' לומר לעכו"ם בין השמשות להדליק נר לצורך שבת [*Shulchan Aruch,* Orach Chayim, 261:1] since, part of the Mitzvah on Shabbos is for there to be light to add to the enjoyment of the meal, as opposed to just lighting in honor of Shabbos).

As a result of *Hadlakah Oseh Mitzvah*, even if our Chanukah candles blow out, the personal act of lighting has already been accomplished and the Mitzvah fulfilled. The Mitzvah is the mere act of lighting — transforming and imbuing with significance that which is normally just a means to an end (i.e., that it should be lit and thereby we should have light). This is because the 'end' — the *Ohr haGanuz* / the Light hidden away at Creation for the 'end of time' — has been revealed in the present moment of lighting the Chanukah lights. Thus, the end becomes revealed in what is normally just the means. In this way, doing becomes being.

ESSAY 3
Publicizing Concealment

PIRSUM HA'NES / TO PUBLICIZE THE MIRACLE, OTHERWISE known as פרסומי ניסא / *Pirsumei Nisa,* is a major theme of Chanukah. This idea and intention informs many of the specific practices we do during Chanukah, including where we place the lights, and why we light lights at all. An exploration of its deeper aspects will illuminate numerous fine points of great spiritual import.

The great Talmudic sage, Rava asks a question: נר חנוכה וקידוש היום מהו קידוש היום עדיף — דתדיר, או דילמא נר חנוכה עדיף — משום פרסומי ניסא? בתר דבעיה, הדר פשטה: נר חנוכה עדיף, משום פרסומי ניסא / "When there is only enough money to buy one or the other, oil for the Chanukah Menorah or wine for Kiddush of Shabbos day, what is the ruling? Does Kiddush of Shabbos day take priority because it is *Tadir* / frequent (it is performed every week, and there is a principle: 'When there is a conflict between a frequent practice and an infrequent practice, the frequent practice takes precedence'), or, perhaps the oil for the Chanukah Menorah takes precedence due to פרסומי ניסא / publicizing the miracle?" He then resolves the dilemma on his own and rules that in this case, the Chanukah Menorah takes precedence due to the issue of publicizing the miracle (*Shabbos*, 23b).

Similarly, נר של חנוכה שהניחה למעלה מעשרים אמה — פסולה / "a Menorah that was placed above 20 *Amos* from the ground is invalid" (*Shabbos*, 22a). Upon this ruling of the Gemara, Rashi writes, דלא שלטא בה עינא למעלה מכ' אמה וליכא פרסומי ניסא / "This is because a person walking with his eyes looking forward does not naturally see what is above 20 Amos, and thus there would be no *Pirsumei Nisa*."

Additionally, we learn in the Baraisa (a parallel text to the Mishnah, *Shabbos*, 21b): נר חנוכה מצוה להניחה על פתח ביתו מבחוץ / "The Mitzvah is to kindle the Chanukah candles at the entrance to one's house on the outside", this too, as Rashi writes, is for the sake of פרסומי ניסא.

Indeed the Menorah should be placed by an exterior door (or window) so that it can be seen and publicized. Yet, the Baraisa continues, ובשעת הסכנה מניחה על שלחנו ודיו / "In a time of danger, one may place it on the table (in the privacy of their home) and that is sufficient to fulfill the obligation."

"In a time of danger" means when there is religious persecution or the like (Rashi and Tosefos), as lighting a Menorah outdoors during such a time could have negative effects. In such a case they should light indoors, on their table and that is sufficient.*

* Regarding a "time of danger": Generally the principle is that נימנו וגמרו בעליית בית נתזה בלוד כל עבירות שבתורה אם אומרין לאדם עבור ואל תהרג יעבור ואל יהרג חוץ מעבודת כוכבים וגילוי עריות ושפיכות דמים / "The sages who discussed this issue counted the votes of those assembled and concluded in the upper story of the house of Nitza in the city of Lod: With regard to all other transgressions in the Torah, if a person is told, "Transgress this prohibition and you will not be killed,' he may transgress that prohibition and not be killed, because the preserving of his own life overrides all of the Torah's prohibitions. This is the

Parallel to these rulings, there is a more theoretical argument among the *Rishonim* / Early Commentators, concerning whether

---

Halacha concerning all prohibitions except for those of idol worship, forbidden sexual relations and bloodshed. Concerning those prohibitions, one must allow himself to be killed rather than transgress them": *Sanhedrin*, 74a. Yet, the Gemara continues, לא שנו אלא שלא בשעת השמד, אבל בשעת השמד - אפילו מצוה קלה יהרג ואל יעבור / "One is permitted to transgress prohibitions in the face of mortal danger only when it is not a time of religious persecution. But in a time of religious persecution, when the gentile authorities are trying to force Jews to violate their religion, even if they issued a decree about a minor Mitzvah, one must be killed and not transgress." The Rambam and the Shulchan Aruch rule this way: *Yorah De'ah*, Siman 157:1. The Rama adds, in the name of the Ran, ודוקא אם רוצים להעבירו במצות לא תעשה אבל אם גזרו גזרה שלא לקיים מצות עשה אין צריך לקיימו ושיהרג ר"ן פרק במה טומנין ונ"י פרק סורר ומורה / "This only refers to prohibitions of the Torah (for example, forcing one to work and desecrate Shabbos), but if the decree is that Jews are not allowed to do positive Mitzvos (such as placing a Mezuzah on a door), then one does not need to be killed and may transgress even during a time of religious persecution." The simple reason, as the Rishonim write (see also, *Chidushei haRamban,* Shabbos, 49a), is that "sitting and not doing" is different than *doing* a transgression, and in any case, in times of religious persecution, if the authorities desire for a Jew not to do a particular positive Mitzvah, they can put the Jew in prison or enforce their edict in such a way that one cannot perform the Mitzvah.

What's more, as the Kli Chemda, writes, when a person is "not doing" the transgression, even if they are killed, G-d forbid, for not doing the transgression, they in fact did not do the transgression. Whereas a person who wishes to perform the positive Mitzvah is caught in the process as they are about to perform the Mitzvah, and put to death, G-d forbid, they in fact did not even perform the Mitzvah, and thus nothing was gained.

Lighting Chanukah candles is a positive Mitzvah, and one from the sages, so why risk one's life by performing this Mitzvah? Perhaps here the "religious persecution" mentioned is not meant as one particular to Klal Yisrael, rather a general decree not to kindle candles during that period. Or, since there is verifiably no real risk involved in lighting discretely inside one's home, this would be an option.

Or perhaps the term *Sha'as haSakana* / time of danger, can mean not just literal persecution, but also some kind of danger or difficulty, such as the candles may blow out if they are outdoors, as the Ritvah explains. Although one could place the candles in a protective glass box to protect them from blowing out, the *Aruch haShulchan* writes that there is no requirement to do so.

the issue of Pirsum haNes is merely an added dimension of the Mitzvah and a preferred way of performing it, or is Pirsum haNes in fact the *Ikar* / main point or *Etzem* / essence of the Mitzvah.

In the Baraisa above, the words of Chazal suggest that the *Mitzvah min-haMuvchar* / the *best* way to do this Mitzvah is to light it by the door, outside with Pirsum haNes; if you cannot, it suffices to light them indoors, even though there is no Pirsum haNes. In other words, Pirsum is the optimal way to perform the Mitzvah, but it is not *essential* to the Mitzvah. The proof of this is that we can perform the Mitzvah even when there is no Pirsum.

Another way of viewing it is that Pirsum is indeed part of the *Ikar* / essence of the Mitzvah of lighting the Chanukah Menorah, however, in a case where it is not possible to light in public and accomplish Pirsum, there is an additional *Takana* / rabbinic injunction, another 'Mitzvah', which is to light it in the home. This second way of understanding the Mitzvah — that Pirsum is the Ikar of the Mitzvah of lighting — seems to be the opinion of the Rambam.

In the Laws of Chanukah, the Rambam begins by giving the historical narrative and backstory for the Chanukah miracle: בבית שני כשמלכי יון גזרו גזרות על ישראל ובטלו דתם ולא הניחו אותם לעסק בתורה ובמצות. ופשטו ידם בממונם ובבנותיהם ונכנסו להיכל ופרצו בו פרצות וטמאו הטהרות. וצר להם לישראל מאד מפניהם ולחצום לחץ גדול עד שרחם עליהם אלהי אבותינו והושיעם מידם והצילם וגברו בני חשמונאי הכהנים הגדולים והרגום והושיעו ישראל מידם והעמידו מלך מן הכהנים וחזרה מלכות לישראל יתר על מאתים שנה עד החרבן השני / "During the period of the Second Temple, when the Greek kings were in power, they proclaimed decrees against the Jewish people, abrogating their religion and forbidding them to study the Torah or to perform the Divine precepts. They laid their hands on their wealth and their daughters; they entered the Temple and broke through it, defiling the things that were pure. The People of Israel were sorely distressed by their enemies, who oppressed them ruthlessly until the G-d of our fathers took pity, saving and rescuing them from the hands of the tyrants. The Chashmona'im, who were great priests, won victories, defeating the Syrian-Greeks and saving Israel from their power. They set up a king from among the priests and Israel's kingdom was restored for a period of more than two centuries, until the destruction of the Second Temple."

And then the Rambam continues: וכשגברו ישראל על אויביהם ואבדום בכ"ה בחדש כסל היה ונכנסו להיכל ולא מצאו שמן טהור במקדש אלא פך אחד ולא היה בו להדליק אלא יום אחד בלבד והדליקו ממנו נרות המערכה שמונה ימים עד שכתשו זיתים והוציאו שמן טהור / "When, on the 25th of Kislev, the Jews had emerged victorious over their foes and destroyed them, they re-entered the Temple where they found only one jar of pure oil, enough to be lit for only a single day; yet they used it for lighting the required set of lamps for eight days, until they managed to press olives and produce pure oil."

Surprisingly, the Rambam offers a historical narrative for Chanukah. This is unlike his normal writing style; he does not give any historical narrative in the laws of Purim or Pesach, for instance. However, in the introduction to the *Mishneh Torah*, the Rambam writes, 'If you read the Tanach and this book, you will have all the practical knowledge you need to live a Torah life.' Nothing about the Chanukah narrative appears in Tanach because Tanach was already canonized and complete at the time of the Chanukah miracle. The story of the miracle must therefore be elaborated here so people will know what Chanukah is about, and have enough "practical" and "contextual" knowledge to meaningfully observe it.

As mentioned, it seems from the writing of the Rambam that he views פרסומי ניסא / revealing the miracle to be an integral part of the essence of the Mitzvah of lighting the Menorah. And it is from this perspective that we can more deeply understand what and how he writes about Chanukah in the *Mishneh Torah.*

In the Rambam, there are two chapters in the laws of Chanukah: Chapter Three, which basically speaks about the miracle of Chanukah and the laws of Hallel, and Chapter Four, where the Rambam focuses on the other main and distinct Mitzvah of Chanukah, the lighting of the Menorah, describing how to light the candles: כמה נרות הוא מדליק בחנכה / "How many lights should one light on Chanukah....?"

Yet, interestingly, in Chapter Three, after offering the history of Chanukah, he continues: ומפני זה התקינו חכמים שבאותו הדור שיהיו שמונת הימים האלו שתחלתן כ"ה בכסלו ימי שמחה והלל ומדליקין בהן הנרות בערב על פתחי הבתים בכל לילה ולילה משמונת הלילות להראות ולגלות הנס / "And because of this our sages established in that generation that these eight days, which begin on the 25th of Kislev, will be days of *Simchah* and *Hallel*, and we also light candles in the evening near the doorposts of our homes on each of these eight nights, to show and reveal the miracle" (*Hilchos Chanukah,* 3:3).

In Chapter Three, when speaking about the lighting of Menorahs, he only needs to say that we light them during this time, since the details of their lighting will be elaborated in Chapter Four. Yet, he nonetheless adds there, ומדליקין בהן הנרות בערב על פתחי הבתים בכל לילה ולילה משמונת הלילות להראות ולגלות הנס / "...and we light candles on our doorsteps each night, *in order to reveal and display the miracle.*"

Why is this detail of candle lighting written in Chapter Three? One might think this is not the right place for this information; it would seem to belong not in the general overview, but in the procedural details. From another perspective, this is proof that להראות ולגלות הנס / revealing the miracle is the *Ikar* / principle element of the Mitzvah, not just an additional or optional detail. It is thus in the category of a general theme or fundamental postulate of Chanukah. The Mitzvah of lighting candles is interwoven with the Mitzvah of making the story of the miracle known to all. In fact it is one Halacha to light for the purpose of Pirsum haNes, and it is a separate Halacha to light in your home if necessary.

So now we know that Pirsum is essential to the lighting of the Menorah, yet the question remains: why? Why the need for, and emphasis on, publicizing the miracle? Why is Chanukah different, for example, than Purim where there is also the idea of Pirsum HaNes, but it does not seem as essential? For instance, regarding Purim there is a law: אמר רב מגילה בזמנה קורין אותה אפי' ביחיד שלא בזמנה בעשרה / "Rav said: 'One may read the Megillah in its proper time, on the 14th of Adar, even privately. However, when it is read not at its proper time, (when the villages advance their reading to the day of assembly), it must be read with a quorum of ten'. רב אסי אמר בין בזמנה בין שלא בזמנה בעשרה הוה עובדא וחש ליה רב להא דרב אסי / Rav Asi says, 'Both in its proper time and not in its proper time there should be a *Minyan* / quorum of ten men.' There was an incident where Rav had to read the Megillah on Purim, and he was concerned regarding this opinion of Rav Asi (and gathered a Minyan)"

(*Megillah,* 5a). In other words, it is always better to read the Megillah with ten, for the purpose of Pirsum haNes (as Rashi writes), yet it is not essential, and certainly one can read the Megillah on Purim in private. And it is not considered two separate Mitzvos to read the Megillah with a Minyan, or to read it by oneself, as is the case with lighting the Chanukah Menorah, as established.

From a certain perspective, it is possible to argue that the reason Pirsum haNes is so essential to Chanukah is for the same reason that the Rambam details the entire history and miracle of Chanukah in the laws of Chanukah: since Chanukah is not recorded in Tanach, and there is no scroll to read on Chanukah, it is entirely upon us to publicize the miracle through our lighting of the Menorah. The act itself is the sacred text, a living word.

It falls to us to publicize and draw attention to the miracle, because people — even if they have read all of Tanach — may not have studied the Oral Torah, and would potentially have no other way of knowing about it. Everyone can read about the miracles of *Yetzias Mitzrayim* / going out of Egypt in the Torah, and similarly, anyone can read about the miraculous events of Purim in the Megillah. But the story of Chanukah *has* to be given over to the people 'orally' by experientially drawing their attention to it.

Yet, there is something even deeper to the idea of Pirsum in its relationship with Chanukah, beyond simply allowing people to know about the miracle that would otherwise not be known. Pirsum is even more intrinsically connected with Chanukah and the Menorah, as we will see.

Tosefos (*Shabbos,* 23b) bring down the opinion that when, within the eight days of Chanukah, Rosh Chodesh Teves falls on Shabbos, the Haftarah should be read from the prophecy of Zecharyah, which talks about the lamps of the Menorah, and not from the normal Rosh Chodesh Shabbos Haftarah. And what is the reason given for this choice of reading — פרסומי ניסא / publicizing the miracle. Interestingly, Tosefos also write that the reading of the Torah during Chanukah, in which we read about the *Korbanos* / offerings that were brought by the *Nesi'im* / the princes of the tribes, describing the *Chanukas haMizbeach* / Dedication of the Altar, does not accomplish פרסומי ניסא since we do not mention candles explicitly, whereas in the Haftarah of Zecharyah we do mention candles. But then the obvious question remains — in the prophecy of Zecharyah, there is of course no mention of the miracle of Chanukah, as it had not happened yet, rather it just mentions the Menorah with its kindled candles in the Beis haMikdash. What then does this reading have to do with Chanukah? Why is the simple mention of candles, even in a different context, considered פרסומי ניסא? True, once we are thinking about candles we are reminded of the candles of Chanukah, but is there פרסומי ניסא inherent in merely mentioning candles themselves?

Furthermore, in Davenning when we recite the insertion *Al haNisim* / "Upon the Miracles..." we describe the battle, but not the miracle of the oil. Although we do mention there that they lit the lamps when they celebrated, the actual miracle is nowhere to be seen. And yet this mention of lighting, according to the sages, is considered an act of Pirsum haNes (משום פרסומי ניסא מדכרינן: *Shabbos*, 24a), even though it perhaps refers to their lighting up of the outer *Chatzer* / courtyard and not actually to the lighting of the Menorah. It would seem from these examples above that there is some inherent connection between the image and act of kindling lights and Pirsum HaNes, even without the historical context of the Chanukah story involved. What is it about candles, fire and flame, that is so interconnected with this concept of Pirsum?

From all the above it is clear that Chanukah is generally related to Pirsum, and Pirsum is specifically related to the lighting of candles. Now on one hand, Pirsum is of course connected to lighting candles because of the miracle, as the Nes occurred with oil and candles, but this itself needs explanation: why should we not do Pirsum haNes with oil alone, such as adding oil to all our foods? Why do we need to use it to light? And the deeper question is, why did the miracle of Chanukah occur with, out of all things, the oil and the Menorah?

REVEALING WITH TZNIYUS

והצנע לכת עם־אלקיך / "Walk humbly with (Hashem) your G-d" (*Michah*, 6:8). והצנע is the Torah root word for *Tzniyus* / modesty, humility, not showing off. Regarding this verse, our sages (*Makos*, 24a) tell us, והצנע לכת זה הוצאת המת והכנסת כלה / "'And to walk humbly with your G-d'— this is an allusion to taking the dead out for burial and accompanying a bride to her wedding canopy (both of which are to be performed without fanfare)." Our sages continue, "If, with regard to matters that tend to be conducted in public (funerals and weddings), the Torah tells us to "walk humbly" when doing them, then in matters that tend to be conducted in private (charity and Torah study), all the more so should they be conducted with Tzniyus."

Interestingly, funerals and weddings are both usually done with large displays of fanfare in public, and even with music or public dancing or public wailing. In the times of Chazal, not only weddings, but funerals also had some form of music played at them. Therefore, when our sages tell us that a wedding and funeral should be done with modesty, inwardness and humility, they are not saying that there shouldn't be any outward expression of one's joy or grief in response to the event, they are saying that *the Pirsum should be done with Tzniyus.*

Normally Pirsum and Tzniyus are thought of as two completely separate qualities. פרסום / public display and להראות ולגלות / 'to show and reveal' stand on one extroverted end of a spectrum, whereas quiet, unassuming hiddenness and humility are on the other introverted end. There is either sound or silence, publicity or privacy, revealing or concealing. And yet, paradoxically, while *Dibbur* / speech and expression, the world of Pirsum, is an integral part of both a wedding and a funeral, these two highly significant life-cycle events need to be performed with Tzniyus.

Regarding a wedding our sages tell us אגרא דבי הלולי — מילי / "The primary reward for participating in a wedding is for the words spoken," namely, the words that bring joy to the groom, such as extolling praises of the bride (*Berachos*, 7b. Rashi), proclaiming what a wonderful bride he has chosen. Similarly, at a funeral, a eulogy is an essential part of the service. This is done not only for the honor of those remaining, the living, but also for the יקרא דשכבי / honor of the deceased (see *Sanhedrin*, 46b). This means that after a person passes on and is beginning their afterlife journey, it is important that we eulogize and publicly praise the person who just passed on, thus giving comfort to their soul and allowing a smoother transition into a higher existence.

In both of these transitional events we need to make our voice heard in order to publicize the honor of the individual, and yet, simultaneously, we need to do so with a sense of Tzniyus, quietness, hiddenness, and inwardness. How can one accomplish Pirsum with Tzniyus, speak with silence, publicize with privacy, reveal with concealment?

True, normal modalities of speech are meant to reveal; inherently words and other forms of expression function in a paradigm of Pirsum and outwardness. Yet, there is a higher or deeper form of speech, emanating from the world of Tzniyus and inwardness. And it is this level of communication that is reflected in the lights of Chanukah.

To go a bit deeper, we can say there are two types of speech. One person speaks solely to expose their thoughts and feelings, to indiscriminately reveal their 'insides' to the outside world. This is pure 'Pirsum' without any sense of privacy; anything private is completely exposed. Another person speaks in a way that reveals something while concealing something else. In fact, when such words are spoken, more than what is being said remains unsaid. Despite the words spoken and the revealing of information to those on the outside, a sacred sense of privacy and honor are still preserved within. One can actually safeguard and even perpetuate a deeper layer of self by revealing something more exterior. Besides, a revelation of *Chitzonius* / externality can indirectly hint at deeper layers of *Penimiyus* / interiority without exposing them fully..

Then, from the words spoken one understands that there is an even deeper truth and inner reality. This is *Pirsum b'Tzniyus* / revealing with modesty, interiority.

In the first paradigm of speech, a person spills everything in their minds, mouths off, and simply empties their thoughts into the 'public domain'. In the second type of speech, the listener is able to recognize that as much as the person is revealing through their words, there are great depths beneath the fountain of their thoughts. By listening deeply to such an expression, you can hear intimations of hidden profundities beneath the surface.

There is a type of revelation which is nakedness, completely exposing to all what is contained within, but there is also a type of revelation that reveals by concealing. This type of disclosure communicates a mystery, a secret, as it is clear that what is being revealed is not the totality of what is present, and the secret thereby remains intact, retaining its mystery.

This is the secret of real Tzniyus. It is not simply covering over or hiding away, rather it is deftly employing a small measure of external Pirsum to hint that there is even more concealed within, all the while cultivating and maintaining a sense of honor, nobility, privacy, and intrigue. This, in fact, is how Hashem reveals Himself through the Torah, in which a story, a law, or even a subtle nuance in the spelling of a word, allows us to understand that there is infinite depth and light concealed beneath the surface of the text. The Black Fire of the holy letters are sacred signs directing us to connect to the White Fire behind, beneath, and within them.

L'Havdil / to mark a distinction, total exposure is cheap and shallow, as nothing remains to be discovered. It merely exposes the fact that there is no interiority, no imagination, no mystery, and no depth present beneath the surface. While over-exposure *seems* to be a revelation, a light, it is actually a form of darkness, as will be explained.

Speaking with Tzniyus at a wedding or funeral, or for that matter in any life situation, means to reveal but not expose, to share oneself but not to empty oneself, to speak words that communicate that there are depths beyond depths behind or within the words that are being spoken. The words themselves simply reveal the presence of a deeper, concealed world within or beyond what is immediately perceivable.

THE PENIMIYUS OF THE WORLD

גוי ששבת חייב מיתה / "An idol-worshiper who keeps Shabbos is liable to death" (*Sanhedrin*, 58b. *Goy* refers to an idol-worshiper: *Beis haOtzar*, Moda'ah in the beginning. See also, Rambam, *Hilchos Ma'achalos Asuros*, 11:8. Although this is not literal — מכין אותו ועונשין אותו ומודיעין אותו שהוא חיב מיתה על זה אבל אינו נהרג: *Hilchos Melachim*, 10:9). What is it specifically about Shabbos, over all other Mitzvos, that warrants a theoretical death penalty for such an appropriation? And what does this have to do with Tzniyus?

Chazal tell us (in *Beitza*, 16a), "Every Mitzvah which Hashem gave to the People of Israel, He gave them publicly — *except Shabbos*, which Hashem bestowed upon them in secret, for it is said, 'It is a sign between Me and the Children of Israel forever'" (*Shemos*, 31: 17).

Shabbos was uniquely transmitted "between Me and the Children of Israel"; it was a transmission of interiority and intimacy, from a place beyond Creation, and thus it was a transmission in utter privacy and hidden mystery. It was a *Penimiyus* / internal transmission, of a Penimiyus reality, to the Penimiyus of a people in touch with and part of the Penimiyus of Creation. Only a people that is essentially beyond the facades of physicality and materialism, and attached to the Living Presence of the Creator, is connected with the world of Shabbos.

In contrast, an idol worshipper subscribes wholesale to the world of *Chitzoniyus* / externality, as an idol is an object that is seen as an end in itself. He is one who worships the 'image', who observes the exterior world as empty of any deeper dimension of Transcendence, and who devotes himself to this degrading, illusory image of reality. As such, if an idol worshiper, one who only connects to the world of the exterior, attempts to connect with the hidden mystery of Shabbos, the inner world of Penimiyus, he ceases to exist (*Beis haOtzar*, Ma'areches, Aleph, 1).

Shabbos is the Penimiyus of the world. Someone who exists only in the world of Chitzoniyus, who tries to connect themselves to the world of Penimiyus, inevitably ceases to exist. This is not necessarily (perhaps only) a literal death sentence, rather, on a deeper level, they simply cannot continue to exist as they have existed up until this point.

סתם עובד כוכבים מפעא פעי / "Ordinary idol worshipers speak loudly" (*Chullin*, 133b). Because idol worshipers are connected to the world of *Chitzoniyus* / externality, they tend to speak loudly. In other words, "loudly" is not merely a quantitative measurement of volume, but also a qualitative energy: their speech is a 'full-voiced' emptying of their inner selves into the outside world. Everything is projected outward and nothing is left private or quiet. Such idolatrous consciousness is constantly ringing with loud and vulgar proclamations of Pirsum, without any sense of hiddenness or Tzniyus (Maharal, *Gur Aryeh*, Shemos, 2:14. *Nesivos Olam*, Nesiv HaShesika, 1).

Most people today are not classical 'idol worshipers', yet, on a more subtle level, sadly, many people do live superficially, in a world of Chitzoniyus. Devotion to material possessions or the ego also constitute subtle (or not-so-subtle) forms of contemporary idolatry. When someone is living superficially, it means they have very little *Penimius* / inner life, and as a result they "speak too loudly" and are always over-exposing themselves with no Tzniyus or sense of self-respect.

Yet, a person who lives authentically and deeply, with a rich inner life, when they do speak in a mode of Pirsum, their Pirsum is expressed with Tzniyus. They therefore speak in such a way that maintains integrity and mystery, while at the same time communicating a tangible sensitivity and respect for what is not being revealed.

If you are a deeper person, and are not swayed by the fads and facades of the world, wherever you look you see that there is something deeper going on, that there is *Elokus* / Divinity present which is not openly revealed, and that there is a perpetual mystery at the heart of existence. The conscious cultivation of this perspective elevates and connects one to the Penimius of all Creation.

A MITZVAH OF REVEALING AND CONCEALING

Now let us return to the topic of Chanukah itself. Every Yom Tov has a *Mitzvas haYom* / special Mitzvah of the day, and this Mitzvah is virtually always done *baYom* / in the daytime, not at night. For example, the Mitzvah of Rosh Hashanah is to blow the Shofar. When do you blow it? During the *Yom*, the day. Similarly, making a blessing over the Lulav on Sukkos is done during the day, and the Mitzvos of Purim, such as delivering gifts and holding a *Seudah* / drinking feast, are done on the day of Purim (*Megilah*, 7b. The *main* reading of the Megilah is by day, והעיקר הוי ביממא. Tosefos, *Megilah*, 4a). If you do any of these Mitzvos while it is still night, you are not *Yotzei* / discharged from your obligation; you have not yet done the Mitzvah.*

We can therefore conclude that Chanukah is the only Yom Tov when the Mitzvas haYom, lighting the candles, is actually done at night, in the darkness. Why this anomaly? Of course, the simple reason is because the miracle itself occurred in the evening, because they lit the Menorah at night, but nothing is mere coincidence and there must be a deeper reason why this unique "Mitzvah of the day"

---

* With regards to Pesach, the Mitzvos today are to eat the Matzah and Maror at night, but that is because Pesach night is called *haLayla* / the night (feminine) *haZeh* / this (masculine, rather than *haZos* / this feminine), as the Shaloh and Gra explain: *Shaloh*, Meseches Pesachim, Ma'aseh. Gra, *Pirush Haggadah*. There is thus an element of 'day' present during the 'night' of Pesach. In fact, we learn that on Pesach night in Mitzrayim we experienced ולילה כיום יאיר / the night shines like day": *Tehilim*, 139:12. *Zohar* 2, 131a. The night (feminine) shone like the day (masculine), to the extent that it was in fact 'day'.

is performed at night.*

Perhaps the resolution is simply that we light at night only because if you light candles in the daylight, their light is insignificant; "A candle in sunlight is superfluous." But our intention with the candles is not to derive utility or pleasure from them, and besides, this is a more Penimi question: why in fact did the miracle of Chanukah occur during the evening, and why is our form of celebrating that miracle performed in the evening? What is the connection between Chanukah, evenings and lighting candles?

THE DARKNESS OF SECULAR, G-DLESS ENLIGHTENMENT

Choshech / darkness represents Yavan, the Greeks. וחשך על־פני תהום / *V'Choshech al P'nei haTehom* / "...And there was darkness on the surface of the depths" (*Bereishis*, 1:2), *Choshech*, says the Medrash, refers to *Galus Yavan* / the Greek Exile (*Medrash Rabbah*, Bereishis, 2:4).

The *Zohar Chadash* (Noach) teaches us that when Noach sends away the *Yonah* / dove and the Yonah comes back to the *Teivah*

* To reinforce this inquiry: according to the Meiri (*Shabbos*, 21b), the battle against the Greeks terminated on the 24th of Kislev, and on that very same night (which according to Torah law is the 25th), they lit the Menorah, thus the first night of Chanukah is the 25th. Yet, the Rambam clearly writes that they were victorious on the 25th, and on the 25th they entered the Beis haMikdash (*Hilchos Chanukah*, 3:2), which would suggest that they lit the Menorah with the miraculous oil on the 26th, so why do we begin Chanukah on the 25th?

It could be argued that this opinion of the Rambam is consistent with his opinion that every morning as well, if the candles went out during the night, they were again lit in the morning (*Hilchos Temidim u'Musafin*, 3:10-12, although, אין מחנכין את המנורה אלא בהדלקת שבעה נרותיה בין הערבים). In this way, they lit the Menorah by day, so why don't we light the Menorah of Chanukah, at least the first night during the day?

/ ark, the Teivah represents the Beis haMikdash. The First Beis haMikdash is the Teivah before the Yonah leaves. The Second Beis haMikdash is the Teivah when the Yonah comes back to it and settles again. But then the Yonah leaves and does not come back to settle, it only carries an *Alei Zayis* / olive leaf. The Third Beis haMikdash is not yet built, but the olive branch represents the oil of Chanukah, which keeps our dreams of redemption burning brightly through the darkness of exile.

ותבא אליו היונה לעת ערב והנה עלה־זית טרף בפיה / "The dove came back to him toward evening, and there in its bill was a plucked-off olive leaf" (*Bereishis*, 8:11). Towards the "evening" refers to the Greek exile, and the "dove" to Klal Yisrael. Holding an olive leaf refers to the miracle with olive oil on Chanukah. By lighting the oil in the Menorah we are able to counter the *Eis Erev* / evening time or darkness of Yavan.

At first glance, darkness is not what one would think characterized the Greeks. They also represent intellectualism, the world of clarity, the light of day. The Greeks worshiped images, and promoted exalting the exposed body for all to see and venerate. Yavan as darkness therefore implies overexposure and the emptying of anything internal, manifesting as crude, superficial intellectualism. In place of deep light, one is left with only a facade, a Chitzoni covering over a lurking darkness. Yavan is thus a blinding light, a clarity that obstructs one's view of what is present beneath that which is physically perceivable; Chanukah, on the other hand, is a visionary darkness, a visceral faith in miracles that transform all natural phenomena into transparent messengers of the Most High.

A contemporary equivalent to the Choshech of Yavan is an unfiltered internet. The internet is full of platforms where people can and are exposing anything and everything of themselves to the world, from sonograms of the fetus growing inside them, to the foods they are eating for each meal, to the stray thoughts they are entertaining at any given moment. The whole premise of such a pursuit is: 'How much attention can I draw to myself; how much can people see and know about me?' Thus, the word 'internet', when spelled in Hebrew as אינטרנט (Aleph/1, Yud/10, Nun/50, Tes/9, Reish/200, Nun/50, Tes/9), has a Gematriya of 329, which is also the value of חשך / *Choshech* (Ches/8, Shin/300, Chaf/20, plus 1 for the *Kollel* / the word itself). This is precisely the devastating darkness of Yavan manifesting in our days; and, as a result, people are not leaving any sacred space for themselves. There is nothing holy, everything is emptied out into the public domain. And, sadly, in place of feeling more connected, as more "sharing" and more "light" is superficially being exposed, people are feeling more alienated, more alone, more frustrated, more depressed, more cut off from one another, and, increasingly, more in the dark.

THE CHANUKAH MIRACLE OCCURS DURING A TIME PERIOD OF META-DARKNESS

Historically, the miraculous events connected to the major *Yamim Tovim* / Holy Days occurred during the age of prophecy and open miracles: the Exodus from Egypt celebrated on Pesach, the Clouds of Glory celebrated on Sukkos, and the giving of the Torah celebrated on Shavuos. As such, the Mitzvos of these Yamim Tovim are performed during the openness and revelation of the daytime, as prophecy is connected to 'light' and the 'day', and they express what 'day' represents. Purim occurs in between the age of prophecy and the age of the sages, between the First and Second Beis haMikdash, between 'day' and 'night', and thus we read the Megilah by day and also by night.

Chanukah is unique in that it occurred in the age of the sages, the era of *Torah she-b'al-Peh* / the oral aspect of Torah. This period parallels (*l'Havdil* / to draw a distinction) the age of Greek dominance and the popularization of Hellenism with its obsession with externality and over-exposure, resulting in Chitzoniyus forms of speech, 'dialogue', and empirical philosophy. Simply put, it was a time of night and darkness, Pirsum without Tzniyus.

Precisely at this time the miracle of Chanukah comes to dispel this surface layer of darkness, and to draw light down into the depths of darkness in order to illuminate it. We therefore perform the Mitzvah of Chanukah at nighttime, as the miracle occurred in the meta-historical time period of 'night', and within the reigning culture of darkness. Our tiny, miraculous lights thus literally and figuratively push aside the overwhelming Choshech of Yavan, revealing the light within the darkness.

Powerfully and poignantly, Chazal harnessed the tools of the Greeks — Pirsum for the sake of Pirsum, exposure as an end in itself — for the purposes of Penimiyus and Transcendence. In contemporary life, Pirsum for the sake of Pirsum means making yourself known for the sake of being known. However, Pirsum can be used for the sake of something deeper, as a means to an end. Chanukah empowers us to use the means of Pirsum to reveal Penimiyus, while always remaining deeply enfolded within Tzniyus.

A flame, by its very definition, is Pirsum: it lights up a room and reveals what is within it. Yet it is also, by nature, Pirsum with Tzniyus. A flame directs attention to everything around it, but not to itself, as it were. It keeps itself concealed. If you look very closely at a flame you will notice that at its center is an emptiness, a 'darkness' or hiddenness that is not being revealed in the radiance of the flame. At its center, in its Penimiyus, there is Tzniyus.

Moreover, while the flame illuminates its surroundings, it also leaps upwards, pointing to something still higher, more mysterious and more hidden, beyond itself.

As above, there is a type of speech which is 'Pirsum only', completely exposing everything inside to the external world, blabbering without restraint. This indicates that there is nothing sacred left within, nothing Penimi, no inner life to be revealed. And yet, there is another kind of speech which is Pirsum b'Tzniyus, revealing for the sake of concealing, or revealing for the sake of others.

The victory of Chanukah is demonstrated in the world of darkness by kindling flames of fire which illuminate everything around them, while still maintaining their core of hiddenness. This is Pirsum b'Tzniyus. And, the purpose of these candles, as explained, is specifically *Pirsum haNes* / revealing the fact that there are miracles and profound, hidden realities in this Divine Creation.

Nes / miracle, the Arizal teaches, has a *Gematriya* / numerical value of 110, which is the same as the words *Mah* / 'What' (45) plus *Ado-noi* (65). A miraculous event causes us to wonder, pause and exclaim, 'What? What just happened?' Our sense of mystery is awakened through a Nes, and we sense the Hand of *Ado-noi* / Hashem within the world.

Pirsum haNes means to reveal that there is mystery within Creation, beyond the predictable and the 'inevitable'. Within and beyond the Laws of Nature, there is the Spirit of the Divine. The Nes of Chanukah reveals that everything is, ultimately, a Nes; every object, event and person is pointing ever higher, toward the infinite depths of reality.

FLICKERING FLAME

Not only is a flame an image that is subtly pointing to or suggesting something else beyond itself, the image of a flame is itself elusive, as it is not static. On one hand, a flame is a defined image, yet its form is continually shifting and fading in and out of perceptibility. Its light flickers in a state of flux between revealing and concealing, alternately 'speaking' and 'being silent'. A flame is in this way a perfect medium to express the nature of miracles, and also to manifest Pirsum with Tzniyus.

Tzniyus does not mean to cover everything, nor to refrain entirely from speech; a better word for that would be *Helem* / concealment. Rather, Tzniyus implies revealing just enough to demonstrate that there is much more that remains concealed.

So while Yavan's darkness is rooted in an exclusive interest in Pirsum for its own self-serving sake, the "spotlight" syndrome, on Chanukah we reveal a more subtle approach to Pirsum, 'Pirsum with Tznyius', publicity which points beyond itself. This approach holds a dynamic tension between openness and closure, objectivity and subjectivity, light and darkness. Weaving and integrating the dichotomies and polarities of life into a complex tapestry that both reveals its beauty and design while also concealing what is vital and essential behind or beneath it, such is the goal of Pirsum b'Tzniyus.

Chazal tell us that Miriam was one of the most beautiful women in history, and that כל הרואה אותה מוליך אתנן לאשתו / "any (man) who saw Miriam would bring a gift to his wife" (*Sotah*, 12a). This is the *Omek* / depth of the idea of Tzniyus. Tzniyus is not just covering oneself, but even what is revealed is not to draw attention to oneself, but rather to draw attention to someone or something else. Miriyam's beauty actually directed a man's attention to the beauty of his own wife; it was Pirsum b'Tzniyus. Miriyam is thus like a candle that illuminates other objects in her proximity, directing attention not to herself, but to others in her sphere of radiance, turning spouses' hearts towards each other in deeper communion.

The opposite of this selfless illumination is the Choshech of Yavan, exposing the body and its powers for its own sake, as in the ancient olympics or commercial advertisement. The Pirsum of the Ohr of Chanukah comes to counter this, helping us to assert that 'My life is here to point to something deeper. It is not always or only about 'me'. And no matter how much I am revealing, it is *Megaleh Tefach uMechaseh T'fachayim* / 'exposing one handbreadth and concealing two', meaning to conceal something much deeper.

"These candles are sanctified, and we have no permission to use them (for anything else), rather just to look at them…." We are therefore bidden to have no utilitarian use for these candles. What then are the candles for, and why do we look at them? *K'dei l'Hodos u-l'Hallel l'Shimcha haGadol* / "...in order to thank and praise Your great Name." These candles thus function to bring us to thank and praise something higher than ourselves, something deeper than our own limited circumstances.

Now we can better understand why the Mitzvah is specifically to light candles *baLayla* / at night, in the *Choshech* / darkness, why the point of doing so is Pirsum haNes, and how Pirsum haNes is achieved specifically through candles. If Chazal had told us that the way to reveal the miracle is to eat Latkes, people would have gotten caught up in the Latke itself; there would have been an inevitable indulgence in the fixed object, a merely static image. The only image that 'exists but does not exist', that implicitly points to something else beyond itself, is a flame.

The Rashba writes that there is a Mitzvah to publicize the fact that someone has done a Mitzvah: מצוה לפרסם עושי מצוה (*Teshuvas haRashba* 1, Siman, 581. Rama, *Yoreh De'ah*, 249:13). For example, it is a Mitzvah to put up a plaque saying that you gave Tzedakah to help build a Beis Medrash. However, this is not to publicize and exalt the individual, rather it is to publicize the Mitzvah and inspire others to give Tzedakah as well.

If you are doing Pirsum to attract attention to yourself, then you are just promoting Choshech, the darkness of Yavan, Chas veShalom. If, like a candle, you are revealing your deeds in order that others will express Hodaah and Hallel to HaKadosh Baruch Hu, or to do goodness and kindness on account of your actions, then you are promoting the intention of Ner Chanukah, you are kindling and revealing the light within the depths of the darkness. Not to dispel the darkness in dualistic fear or rejection, but to illuminate the hidden depths of darkness itself. This is the redemption of the 36 lights and the eight days of Chanukah.

ESSAY 4
Overcoming Forgetfulness

In general, we feel that *shich'cha* / forgetfulness is a curse. As some people grow older, for example, they feel more scattered and begin to forget things, attributing this to 'the curse of aging'. Yet, as the *Chovos haLevavos* (Sha'ar haBechina, 5) and Rabbeinu Yona point out, it is actually a *Chesed* / kindness that HaKadosh Bruch Hu created our brains in such a way that we forget. Imagine if you lived with complete recall of everything you had ever experienced. Imagine if every tragedy we have ever known was constantly present before our eyes as if it was happening in the present moment, or even if every past joy was crowding out our present experience. We would simply not be able to go on living our lives moment to moment.

We learn that Rav Zeira fasted 100 fasts in order to forget what he had learned previously in Bavel, before he went to learn in Eretz Yisrael where there was a higher form of learning (*Baba Metzia*, 85a). Perhaps, he also realized that if everything he learned in the future would only be based on what he had already learned, he would never be able to truly learn anything new. This is an example of healthy forgetfulness. Yet, of course, there is also a negative side of forgetfulness, simply forgetting what one has learned. And more devastatingly, there is a harsher form of forgetfulness which can cause one to lose touch with who they truly are and what their purpose is.

וחשך על־פני תהום / *V'Choshech al P'nei haTehom* / "...And there was darkness on the surface of the depths" (*Bereishis*, 1:2). As mentioned previously, the term *Choshech* here refers to *Galus Yavan* / the Greek Exile. This is also the *Choshech* / darkness of *Shich'cha* / forgetting. In fact, the word *Shich'cha* comes from the word *Choshech*. And so we can understand forgetting as a form of psycho-spiritual darkness.

It was a dark time, indeed, during which the Greeks tried to cause us להשכיחם תורתך / *l'Hashkicham Torasecha* / "to forget Your Torah". More precisely, it was the *Torah she-b'al-Peh* / the Oral Torah, our people's living memory, that they sought to erase, for this was the antithesis to Greek Philosophy.

To over-simplify the basis of Greek Philosophy, its central message was, 'what you see is what you get'; this physical world is an end in itself. The Written Torah reveals the presence of transcendence within the world and within our lives, and the Oral Torah reveals how we can live in a way that engages and amplifies this transcendence, ultimately transforming the world and our lives into a dwelling place for the Divine. The battle of Chanukah was, in this way, a battle in defense of the truth of the Oral Torah, as explored earlier.

And so the question is, if the Kelipah of the Greeks was to cause Klal Yisrael להשכיחם תורתך, to make them forget Your Torah, why is it that we celebrate Chanukah only by saying a blessing and lighting a *Ner* / candle? It would seem that in establishing Chanukah our sages should have added the story of its events to the Written Torah. And if not adding to *Tanach* / the 24 canonized books of the Written Torah, as in how the Purim story was added to the canon, at least our sages might have added a 'Megilas Chanukah', to enshrine the Chanukah story and to have us celebrate Chanukah with its recitation.

And if they could not create a new book of Tanach or a 'Megillah" since it was historically too late for that, as it was no longer the age of prophecy, why did they not at least create a tractate of Oral Torah for Chanukah — the Holy Day most clearly celebrating the victory of the Oral Torah and a victory over להשכיחם תורתך?

In other words; How does merely lighting a few candles counter the anti-Torah ideology of Yavan? Why is our response to להשכיחם תורתך, possibly forgetting Hashem's Torah, an action, rather than a text? One would think that the response should be a 'remembrance' of what they wanted us to forget, and specifically through the medium of Torah, our people's collective memory bank. Should we not use Torah against the darkness of Yavan, rather than a Mitzvah, a mere fleeting, physical act?

True, the *Gematriya* / numerical value of נר חנוכה / *Ner Chanukah* is 339, the same as ישכח / to forget (338 plus the *Kollel* / '1' for the word itself, equals 339), but the question is how does this work? How do we battle the world of forgetfulness with a Mitzvah?

NER = MITZVAH; OHR = TORAH

כי נר מצוה ותורה אור / *Ki Ner Mitzvah v'Torah Ohr* / "A Mitzvah is a lamp and Torah is light" (*Mishlei*, 6:23). "This verse associates the Mitzvah with a lamp and the Torah with the light of the sun. The Mitzvah is associated with a *Ner* / lamp in order to tell you: 'Just as a lamp does not protect one by its light in perpetuity but only temporarily (i.e., while the lamp is in one's hand), so too, a Mitzvah protects one only temporarily (while one is performing the Mitzvah).' And the Torah is associated with *Ohr* / light in order to tell you: 'Just as the light of the sun protects one forever, so too, the Torah one studies protects one forever'" (*Sotah*, 21a). Torah is eternal, a light that shines continuously. By contrast, a Mitzvah is similar to a candle in one's hand; it shines while one is holding it, but in itself it has a short life-span, and it is constantly flickering, revealing or concealing itself at any moment. It also has the potential to be extinguished and thus revert to darkness. Like sunlight during the day, the Torah's Light is constantly present.

In our context, in the world of *Ohr* / light, there is no possibility for darkness, meaning forgetfulness, as everything is always revealed and clear. Whereas in the world of *Ner* / lamp, there is perpetual flickering and a corresponding potential for extinguishing or forgetting of its light.

Within the Torah itself there is *Torah she-b'Ksav* / Written Torah, and *Torah she-b'al-Peh* / an oral aspect of Torah, which is meant to be memorized. These correspond to how the Torah is revealed in the First *Luchos* / Tablets and the way the Torah is revealed in the Second Luchos. "Had Israel not sinned they would have been given the Five Books of the Torah and the book of Yehoshua alone" (*Nedarim*, 22b). In other words, there would have just been 'six books of the Torah' (in the place of the six Sedarim of the Mishnah: *Ben Yehoyada*, ad loc).

Torah she-b'Ksav is the Torah of Ohr, like the sunlight. If there had never been a *Cheit haEigel* / Sin of the Golden Calf, we would have just the *Luchos Rishonos* / the First Tablets, Torah she-b'Ksav. Then, the Torah would have been revealed only on the level of 'Torah Ohr', the constant light, always revealed and before us in total clarity.

The first set of Luchos was inscribed from one side to the other, through and through (*Yerushalmi*, *Shekalim*, 6:1). The truth and light of the Torah permeated these Luchos completely, leaving no room for concealment, darkness or forgetfulness. The revelation of Divine Light on this level has no room for refutation or forgetting, it is quite simply, incontrovertible. The Alter Rebbe explains (*Tanya*, Kuntres Acharon, 6), that forgetfulness is connected to a reality of *Achorayim* / the back or behind, a kind of cosmic 'dark side', and as the First Luchos were inscribed "through and through", there was no back side at all; only pure transparency.

With the event of the Cheit haEigel and the smashing of the Luchos Rishonos, the possibility of 'forgetting' became a reality. From that point on, we were based in a paradigm of the Broken Luchos, in which forgetting and disconnection from ultimate truth is an ever-present danger, and thus there was a corresponding emergence of the Torah she-b'al-Peh, to counteract this encroaching darkness.

אלמלי לא נשתברו לוחות הראשונות — לא נשתכחה תורה מישראל/ "Had the first Luchos not been broken, the Torah would never have been forgotten from the Jewish people" (*Eiruvin*, 54a). There would have only been the uncontested reality of light and revelation, a collective and individual state of total recall, with no possibility of doubt, uncertainty, or even questions.

In other words, in this new paradigm of Broken Luchos, the Torah is now to us like a Ner, flickering like the fragile light of a small candle, sometimes revealed, sometimes not. And it is up to us to kindle and keep that light lit throughout the darkness of the world. When we learn Torah, we are therefore 'remembering what we have forgotten', bringing all the pieces of the broken Luchos back together, gathering the scattered sparks of light back into crystallized wholeness. This is the principle of the Oral Tradition: a perpetual dance of forgetting and remembering. This Divine dialectic is reflected in the idea that we learn the whole Torah in the womb, where there is a נר דלוק לו על ראשו / "a Ner above our head, and we gaze from one end of the world to another, but before being born, an angel removes it from us" (*Niddah*, 30b), and we then proceed to remember fragments of this forgotten Torah throughout our life of learning.

MEMORY BEYOND FORGETFULNESS VS. MEMORY IN A PLACE OF FORGETFULNESS

There is memory which is so revealed and present, that there is no possibility for forgetfulness. This is the Ohr of the First Luchos, and in general, Torah she-b'Ksav. But in truth this cannot be called 'memory', rather it is pure, constant 'revelation', as memory can only exist in a world where it is possible to forget.

When there is full revelation, there is no memory. On one level, this is ideal, as the Divine reality expressed in the Torah is always before one in an effortless and unobstructed way. However, that is a more appropriate level of awareness for angels, who have no freewill and are beyond the world of duality and death. As such, when we received the first set of Luchos we became 'free' from the *Yetzer haRa* / inclination toward negativity (*Zohar* 3, 97b), and thus no longer functioned in a world of freewill or even mortality (we became free from the Angel of Death. *Medrash Rabbah,* Shemos, 41). For human beings to maintain their Divinely gifted freewill, there must be the possibility to forget. Torah is the light of the world, but memory is the light of our mind. If we were incapable of forgetting, we would never need to turn on and develop the light of our mind. In the full exposure of ever-present light, we actually lose our own capacity to create and kindle light. Without forgetting, there is no thinking or learning, and no Torah she-b'al-Peh.

Parenthetically, this is the deeper reason why the word 'internet', written in Hebrew, אינטרנט is Gematriya 329 (Aleph/1, Yud/10, Nun/50, Tes/9, Reish/200, Nun/50, Tes/9), which is the same value as the word שכח / forget (328 plus 1 for the word itself = 329). When all you have to do is a Google search, you do not need to use your mind to remember anything; there's no memory. If you only use Waze to get around, you will not actually know how to get anywhere. In effect, you know nothing because you know everything, without needing to remember. When knowing information is passive, there's no real memory or learning. Memory only exists when there is a possibility of forgetting, and when there's an active process of *establishing* memory, which is a creative act.

Furthermore, remembering is an active process that is relative to forgetting. As the sages teach, אין אדם עומד על דברי תורה אלא אם כן נכשל בהן / "A person does not establish Divrei Torah except by first stumbling in them" (*Gittin*, 43a). You only truly understand something when you first 'stumbled' in it; it was broken and obscured, you forgot, you asked and probed, and now you remember — now it is a part of you, shining within you, not just on or in front of you from without. True ownership of life and of Torah, when the Torah becomes "our Torah" (as in Torah *b'al-Peh*, memorized Torah), occurs when you stumble, when you forget and then learn from your mistakes.

"Stumbling" or forgetting must precede the act of "establishing" or remembering. If you never stumble or forget, you cannot develop or establish memory. This is the essence of Torah she-b'al-Peh, the stumbling, the questioning, the darkness, the uncertainty, — matched by the effort of clarifying, repeating, internalizing and probing, which paves the way for the revelation of ever deeper answers and resolutions, repairs and reconnections. This is how one kindles the light of the memory through the process of Torah she-b'al-Peh.

This is why the story of Chanukah is specifically not written down, not even in a tractate of Gemara. What is the antidote to *l'Hashkicham Torasecha*? Remembering. But if you write something down, you are no longer 'remembering' it; it is then clear, it is always present before you. You can, in effect, forget about it. If someone tells you something 'orally' and asks you to remember it, you will respond by actively preserving it in your memory. We only remember in a place where there is the potential for forgetting; Torah she-b'al-Peh thus exists only when there is a potential for forgetting the Torah. And this is why Chazal established the Mitzvah of kindling a Ner as a symbol of overcoming the Shich'cha of the Greeks, as a Ner always has the potential for being extinguished. In this way, we can understand that every year when we light the Menorah, we are teaching and relearning the oral Torah of Chanukah, as our actions inscribe the light into the tablets of our heart.

In light of the above, it is possible to posit that there are four levels of memory and forgetting:

1. Everything is revealed; there is no possibility of forgetting. This is the Torah she-b'Ksav, a status beyond memory, and hence beyond thought, learning, or freewill.

2. Remembering what was forgotten, in which there remains a potential for forgetting. This is the Torah she-b'al-Peh, a place of memory and learning.

3. Completely forgetting, in which there is no longer a potential for remembering, as one does not even have a memory of forgetting something. This is what Yavan wanted: *l'Hashkicham Torasecha,* a place of total forgetfulness and erasure.

4. Encrypted forgetting; one has a memory of having forgotten something. There is a *Reshimu* / imprint or residue of the information from which memory can be rekindled. This is the flickering Ner Chanukah that overcomes the Choshech of Yavan. It is a state that exists between forgetfulness and memory, but when focused and held in attention, it can rekindle full memory.

When Yaakov is leaving *HaMakom* / the Place, the essence of all space where he dreamt of a mystical ladder, he desires to return there, so he erects a *Matzevah* / monument of stone and pours oil over it (*Bereishis*, 28:18). Oil is *Oseh Rishum* / it creates a residue, as the Rishonim explain (Rasag, Radak, Rabbeinu Bachaye: כי השמן על גבי האבן רשומו ניכר. See also Rashash, *Nahar haShalom*). If you pour a cup of water on the floor and then mop it up, it completely disappears without a *Reshimu* / residue, imprint, and you can forget that it ever happened. If you pour a cup of oil over the floor, it can leave an indelible stain; there's a Reshimu reminding you that something has happened. This is how memory works. We can only remember something when there is a 'residue' indicating that something happened but was forgotten. You need to see, hear, smell, taste or feel something that can remind you of something else, forgotten but not forever lost. This is a deeper meaning of the oil of the Ner Chanukah, it can help us light the way back to our innermost point of truth and clarity.

Chazal say (*Yerushalmi, Shekalim*, 2:5), אין עושין נפשות לצדיקים דבריהם הן הן זכרונן / "One does not make gravestones for the righteous; their words are their remembrance." This is the Halacha recorded by the Rambam (*Hilchos Avel*, 4:4), and *Divreihem* / "their words" refers to *Divrei Torah* / expressions of Torah wisdom. On an inner level, to remember who a Tzadik really is we do not need to rely on knowing where they are buried, the dates of their life-span, or descriptions of their personality. Their words of Torah are still alive. When a person who is not a Tzadik passes away, however, you need to create a *Tziyon* / marker or sign that will memorialize them, a Reshimu to help remember who that person was. A Tziyon is only needed when there are no living words of Divrei Torah.

What happens when the Choshech of Yavan causes us to forget the light of 'Divrei Torah'? We need to create a marker or sign, a Reshimu, so we can remember what we once knew. We need to awaken and activate the Torah imprinted within. The reason we use a Ner as the Mitzvah of Chanukah is that a Mitzvah can serve as such a marker and reminder of Divrei Torah. Built into the Mitzvah is a reminder that we should not allow ourselves *l'Hashkicham Torasecha* / to forget Your Divine Wisdom.

ושמתם את־דברי אלה על־לבבכם ועל־נפשכם / "...and you shall impress these My words upon your very heart and soul" (*Devarim*, 11:18). Says the *Medrash Sifrei* (and Rashi ad loc), "Even after you have been banished from the Land of Israel, make yourselves a Tziyon by means of My commandments: lay Tefillin on your arms and head, attach Mezuzos to your doorposts, so that these shall not be novelties to you when you return to the Land." When we are exiled from our land, and we do not have a living memory of what it means to serve HaKadosh Baruch Hu in its highest, deepest form, we still have the Mitzvos as a Tziyon, to perpetually refresh and firmly reestablish our powers of memory until the redemption from this final exile finally arrives.

In this place of darkness and of exile, with its ever-present potential for forgetfulness, we have already begun to lose the vivid memory of *Geulah* / redemption. Our collective memory of how the Shechinah was revealed in the world and of what it was like to have a Beis haMikdash has begun to fade. We need Mitzvos, actual physical practices, as points of remembrance and reawakening.

Storytelling, studying and memorizing are all important tools to maintain memories of the past, but what truly ensures the survival of sacred memory are dedicated actions, rituals and Mitzvos. Sacred actions imprint every level of our being, including our bodies. Such whole-self devotion inscribes Torah within our cellular memories, a calligraphy of light hidden within, just waiting to be reignited. When memory is distant and virtually lost, it is the power of a meaning-loaded action, the sacred act of a Mitzvah, which maintains memory, or at least a Reshimu of it. This, in turn, allows for a transmission of the living memory of the people to the next generation; not just ideas and values, actual deeds and experiences. Long after it is 'forgotten', a childhood memory can be re-evoked and re-lived through a particular *Minhag* / custom or manner of performing a Mitzvah. Such a practice opens up the individual and allows them to gradually recall something of the fullness of that memory, and ultimately to bring complete remembrance to the surface.

As such, the essential way we celebrate Chanukah, in order to counter the Shich'cha of Yavan and the Shich'cha of this modern world, is performing Mitzvos, and particularly the Mitzvah of kindling a Ner.

IMPRINT OF THE PAST & OF THE FUTURE

Normally, a Reshimu works to awaken memories of the past in the present. Let's say you spilled some oil and forgot about it. You no longer have the oil nor a memory of it, but you still have the mark of the residue, and this can serve as a sign to reconstitute your memory of the spill, including any related lessons or insights you wanted to recall along with it. Memory is the recovery of knowledge of something in the past. Yet, in the world of *Elokus* / Divinity, the dimensionless, eternal world of Infinity, a Reshimu can work in the opposite way as well. A Mitzvah that you are going to do in the future can actually have a Reshimu upon the present. This is why in the *Sifrei haSod*, the 'deeper readings' of Chanukah, Chanukah is not just an imprint from the past, but more powerfully, it is also an imprint and reminder of what is going to happen in the future; illumination of and within darkness itself. Chanukah comes from the word *Chinuch* / education because it is teaching us and triggering our memory of what will be in the future. The 36 lights of Chanukah give us a glimpse of what the world looks like through the eyes of redemption.

May we merit this Chanukah to experience the perfected future within the darkness of the present, with the revealing of Moshiach and the ushering in of the Final Redemption, speedily in our days, Omein.

Other Books by the Author

RECLAIMING THE SELF

The Way of Teshuvah

Teshuvah is one of the great gifts of life. It speaks of a hope for a better today and empowers us to choose a brighter tomorrow. But what exactly is Teshuvah? How does it work? How can we undo our past and how do we deal with guilt? And what is healthy regret without eroding our self-esteem? In this fascinating and empowering book, the path for genuine transformation and a way to include all of our past in the powerful moment of the now, is explored and demonstrated.

THE MYSTERY OF KADDISH

Understanding the Mourner's Kaddish

The Mystery of Kaddish is an in-depth exploration into the Mourner's Prayer. Throughout Jewish history, there have been many rites and rituals associated with loss and mourning, yet none have prevailed quite like the Mourner's Kaddish Prayer, which has become the definitive ritual of mourning. The book explores the source of this prayer and deconstructs the meaning to better understand the grieving process and how the Kaddish prayer supports and uplifts the bereaved through their own personal journey to healing.

UPSHERNISH: The First Haircut

Exploring the Laws, Customs & Meanings of a Boy's First Haircut

What is the meaning of Upsherin, the traditional celebration of a boy's first haircut at the age of three? Why is a boy's hair allowed to grow freely for his first three years? What is the deeper import of hair in all its lengths and varieties? What is the meaning of hair coverings? Includes a guide to conducting an Upsherin ceremony.

A BOND FOR ETERNITY

Understanding the Bris Milah

What is the Bris Milah – the covenant of circumcision? What does it represent, symbolize and signify? This book provides an in depth and sensitive review of this fundamental Mitzvah. In this little masterpiece of wisdom – profound yet accessible —the deeper meaning of this essential rite of passage and its eternal link to the Jewish people, is revealed and explored.

REINCARNATION AND JUDAISM

The Journey of the Soul

A fascinating analysis of the concept of Gilgul / Reincarnation. Dipping into the fountain of ancient wisdom and modern understanding, this book addresses and answers such basic questions as: What is reincarnation? Why does it occur? And how does it affect us personally?

INNER RHYTHMS

The Kabbalah of MUSIC

Exploring the inner dimension of sound and music, and particularly, how music permeates all aspects of life. The topics range from Deveikus/Unity and Yichudim/Unifications, to the more personal issues, such as Simcha/Happiness and Marirus/ sadness.

MEDITATION AND JUDAISM

Exploring the Jewish Meditative Paths

A comprehensive work encompassing the entire spectrum of Jewish thought, from the sages of the Talmud and the early Kabbalists to the modern philosophers and Chassidic masters. This book is both a scholarly, in-depth study of meditative practices, and a practical, easy to follow guide for any person interested in meditating the Jewish way.

TOWARD THE INFINITE

A book focusing exclusively on the Chassidic approach to meditation known as Hisbonenus. Encompassing the entire meditative experience, it takes the reader on a comprehensive and engaging journey through this unique practice. The book explores the various states of consciousness that a person encounters in the course of the meditation, beginning at a level of extreme self-awareness and concluding with a state of total non-awareness.

THIRTY - TWO GATES OF WISDOM
into the Heart of Kabbalah & Chassidus

What is Kabbalah? And what are the differences between the theoretical, meditative, magical and personal Kabbalistic teachings? What are the four paths of interpreting the teachings of the ARIzal? What did Chassidus teach? These are some of the fundamental issues expanded upon in this text. And then, more specifically, why are there so many names of G-d and what do they represent? What are the key concepts of these deeper teachings?

The book explores the grand narrative of the great chain of reality, how there was and is a movement from the Infinite Oneness of Hashem to a world of (apparent) duality and multiplicity.

THE PURIM READER

The Holiday of Purim Explored

With a Persian name, a masquerade dress code and a woman as the heroine, Purim is certainly unusual amongst the Jewish holidays. Most people are very familiar with the costumes, Megilah and revelry, but are mystified by their significance. This book offers a glimpse into the hidden world of Purim, uncovering these mysteries and offering a deeper understanding of this unique holiday.

EIGHT LIGHTS

8 Meditations for Chanukah

What is the meaning and message of Chanukah? What is the spiritual significance of the Lights of the Menorah? What are the Lights telling us? What is the deeper dimension of the Dreidel? Rav Pinson, with his trademark deep learning and spiritual sensitivity guides us through eight meditations relating to the Lights of the Menorah, the eight days of Chanukah, and a fascinating exploration of the symbolism and structure of the Dreidel. Includes a detailed how-to guide for lighting the Chanukah Menorah.

THE IYYUN HAGADAH

An Introduction to the Haggadah

In this beautifully written introduction to Passover and the Haggadah, we are guided through the major themes of Passover and the Seder night. This slim text, addresses the important questions, such as: What is the big deal of Chametz? What are we trying to achieve through conducting a Seder? What's with all that stuff on the Seder Plate? And most importantly, how is this all related to freedom?

PASSPORT TO KABBALAH

A Journey of Inner Transformation

Life is a journey full of ups and downs, inside-outs, and unexpected detours. There are times when we think we know exactly where we want to be headed, and other times when we are so lost we don't even know where we are. This slim book provides readers with a passport of sorts to help them through any obstacles along their path of self-refinement, reflection, and self-transformation.

THE FOUR SPECIES

The Symbolism of the Lulav & Esrog

The Four Species have inspired countless commentaries and traditions and intrigued scholars and mystics alike. In this little masterpiece of wisdom both profound and practical - the deep symbolic roots and nature of the Four Species are explored. The Na'anuim, or ritual of the Lulav movement, is meticulously detailed and Kavanos,, are offered for use with the practice. Includes an illustrated guide to the Lulav Movements.

THE BOOK OF LIFE AFTER LIFE

What is a soul? What happens to us after we physically die?

What is consciousness, and can it survive without a physical brain?

Can we remember our past lives?

Do near-death experiences prove immortality?

What is Gan Eden? Resurrection?

Exploring the possibility of surviving death, the near-death experience and a glimpse into what awaits us after this life.

(This book is an updated and expanded version of the book; Jewish Wisdom of the Afterlife)

THE GARDEN OF PARADOX:

The Essence of Non - Dual Kabbalah

This book is a Primer on the Essential Philosophy of Kabbalah presented as a series of 3 conversations, revealing the mysteries of Creator, Creation and Consciousness. With three representational students, embodying respectively, the philosopher, the activist and the mystic, the book, tackles the larger questions of life. Who is G-d? Who am I? Why do I exist? What is my purpose in this life? Written in clear and concise prose, the text, gently guides the reader towards making sense of life's paradoxes and living meaningfully.

BREATHING & QUIETING THE MIND

Achieving a sense of self-mastery and inner freedom demands that we gain a measure of hegemony over our thoughts. We learn to choose out thoughts so that we are not at the mercy of whatever belches up to the mind. Through quieting the mind and conscious breathing we can slow the onrush of anxious, scattered thinking and come to a deeper awareness of the interconnectedness of all of life.

Source texts are included in translation, with how-to-guides for the various practices.

VISUALIZATION AND IMAGERY:

Harnessing the Power of our Mind's Eye

We assume that what we see with our eyes is absolute. Yet, beyond our ability to choose what we see, we have the ability to choose how we see. This directly translates into how we experience life. In a world saturated with visual imagery, our senses are continuously assaulted with Kelipa/empty/fantasy imagery that we would not necessarily choose. These images can negatively affect our relationship with ourselves, with the world around us, and with the Divine. This volume seeks to show us how we can alter that which we observe through harnessing the power of our mind's eye, the inner sanctum of our imagination. We thus create a new way to see and experience the world. This book teaches us how to utilize visualization and imagery as a way to develop our spiritual sensitivity and higher intuition, and ultimately achieve Deveikus/Unity with Hashem.

SOUND AND VIBRATION:
Tuning into the Echoes of Creation

Through our perception of sound and vibration we internalize the world around us. What we hear, and how we process that hearing, has a profound impact on how we experience life. What we hear can empower us or harm us. A defining human capacity is to harness the power sound -- through speech, dialogue, and song, and through listening to others. Hearing is primary dimension of our existence. In fact, as a fetus our ears were the first fully operating sensory organs to develop.

This book will guide you in methods of utilizing the power of sound and vibration to heal and maintain mental, emotional and spiritual health, to fine-tune your Midos and even to guide you into deeper levels of Deveikus / conscious unity with Hashem. The vibratory patterns of the Aleph-Beis are particularly useful portals into our deeper conscious selves. Through chanting and deep listening, we can use the letters and sounds to shift our very mindset, to induce us into a state of presence and spiritual elevation.

THE POWER OF CHOICE:
A Practical Guide to Conscious Living

It is the essential premise of this book that we hold the key to unlock many of the gates that seem closed to us and keep us from living our fullest life. That key we all hold is the power to choose. The Power of Choice is the primary tool that we have at our disposal to impact the world and effect change within our own lives. We often give up this power to outside forces such as the market, media, politicians or peer pressure; or to internal forces that often function beyond our conscious control such as ego, anger, lust, greed or jealousy. Making conscious, compassionate and creative decisions is the cornerstone of living a mature and meaningful life.

MYSTIC TALES FROM THE EMEK HAMELECH

Mystic Tales of the Emek HaMelech, is a wondrous and inspiring collection of stories culled from the Emek HaMelech. Emek HaMelech, from which these stories have been taken, (as well as its author) is a bit of a mystery. But like all good mysteries, it is one worth investigating. In this spirit the present volume is being offered to the general public in the merit and memory of its saintly author, as well as in the hopes of introducing a vital voice of deeper Torah teaching and tradition to a contemporary English speaking audience

---

INNER WORLDS OF JEWISH PRAYER
A Guide to Develop and Deepen the Prayer Experience

While much attention has been paid to the poetry, history, theology and contextual meaning of the prayers, the intention of this work is to provide a guide to finding meaning and effecting transformation through the prayer experience itself.

Explore: *What happens when we pray? *How do we enter the mind-state of prayer? *Learning to incorporate the body into the prayers. *Discover techniques to enhance and deepen prayer and make it a transformative experience.

This empowering and inspiring text, demonstrates how through proper mindset, preparation and dedication, the experience of prayer can be deeply transformative and ultimately, life-altering.

WRAPPED IN MAJESTY
Tefillin - Exploring the Mystery

Tefillin, the black boxes and leather straps that are worn during prayer, are curiously powerful and mysterious. Within the inky black boxes lie untold secrets. In this profound, passionate and thought-provoking text, the multi-dimensional perspectives of Tefillin are explored and revealed. Magically weaving together all levels of Torah including the Peshat (literal observation), to Remez (allegorical), to Derush, (homiletic), to Sod (hidden) into one beautiful tapestry. Inspirational and instructive, Wrapped in Majesty: Tefillin, will make putting on the Tefillin more meaningful and inspiring.

SECRETS OF THE MIKVAH:
Waters of Transformation

A Mikvah is a pool of water used for the purpose of ritual immersion; a place where one moves from a state of Tumah; impurity, blockage and death—to a place of Teharah; purity, fluidity and life.

In SECRETS OF THE MIKVAH, Rav Pinson delves into the transformative powers of the Mikvah with his trademark all-encompassing perspective that ranges from the literal, Pshat observation and Halachic implications of the texts, to the allegorical, the philosophical, and finally, to the deep secrets of the

Mikvah as revealed by Kabbalah and Chassidus.

This insightful and inspirational text demonstrates how immersion in a Mikvah can be a transformative and life-altering practice, and includes various Kavanos—deep intentions—for all people, through various stages of life, that empower and enrich the immersion experience.

THE SPIRAL OF TIME:

A 12 Part Series on the Months of the Year.

The following titles from the series are now available!

THE SPIRAL OF TIME:

Unraveling the Yearly Cycle

Many centuries ago, the Sages of Israel were the foremost authority in the fields of both astronomical calculation and astrological wisdom, including the deeper interpretations of the cycles and seasons. Over time, this wisdom became hidden within the esoteric teachings of the Torah, and as a result was known only to students and scholars of the deepest depths of the tradition. More recently, the great teachers, from R.Yitzchak Luria (the Arizal) to the Baal Shem Tov, taught that as the world approaches the Era of Redemption, it is a Mitzvah / spiritual obligation to broadly reveal this wisdom.

"The Spiral of Time" is volume 1 is a series of 12 books, and serves as an introductory book to the basic concepts and nature of the Hebrew calendar and explores the special day of Rosh Chodesh.

THE MONTH OF SHEVAT: ELEVATING EATING

& The Holiday of Tu b'Shevat

Each month of the year radiates with a distinct Divine energy and thus unique opportunities for growth, *Tikkun* and illumination. According to the deeper teachings of the Torah, all of these distinct qualities, opportunities and natural phenomena correspond to a certain data set. That is, the nature of each month is elucidated by a specific letter of the Aleph Beis, a tribe, verse, human sense, and so forth. The month of Shevat is particularly connected to food and our relationship to bodily intake. During this month we celebrate Tu b'Shevat, the New Year of the Tree, and aspire to create a proper and physically/emotionally/spiritually healthy relationship with food.

THE MONTH OF ADAR:
Transformation Through Laughter & Holy Doubt

Each month of the year radiates with distinct Divine qualities and unique opportunities for growth and spiritual illumination. As Adar concludes the monthly cycle of the year, as well as the solar phenomena of the winter, it is an appropriate month to think about our essential identity, before moving out to meet the world come spring. This month we strive to create a healthy relationship with holy humor, unbounded joy, and a general sense of lightness of being. Through the work of Adar we transform negative, crippling doubt and uncertainties into radical wonderment and openness.

THE MONTH OF IYYAR: EVOLVING THE SELF
& The Holiday of LAG B'OMER

The month of IYYAR is the second month of the spring, a month that connects the Redemption from Egypt in Nissan with the Revelation of Torah in Sivan. The Chai/ Eighteenth day of the Month is the day we celebrate the Rashbi (Rabbi Shimon Bar Yochai) and the revealing of the hidden aspects of the Torah. This is the 'Holiday' of Lag b'Omer. The book explores the unique quality of this special month, a month that has a Mitzvah of counting the Omer every day. In addition, the book explores the roots and significance of the mystical 'holiday' of Lag b'Omer. Including the customs & Practices of Lag b'Omer, such as, bonfires, bows & arrows, parades, Upsherin, and more.

THE MONTHS OF TAMUZ AND AV:

Embracing Brokenness - 17th of Tamuz, Tisha B'Av, & Tu B'Av

Each month and season of the year, radiates with distinct Divine qualities and unique opportunities for growth and Tikkun.

The summer month of Tamuz and Av contain the longest and hottest days of the year. The raised temperature is indicative of a corresponding spiritual heat, a time of harsher judgement and potential destruction, such as the destructions of the first and second Beis HaMikdash, which began on the 17th of Tamuz and culminated on the 9th and 10th of Av.

A few days later, on Tu b'Av, the darkness is transformed and reveals the greatest light and possibility for new life. During these summer months of Tamuz and Av we embrace our brokenness so that we can heal and transform darkness into light.

THE MONTH OF ELUL:

Days of Introspection and Transformation

Each month of the year radiates with a distinct quality and provides unique opportunities for growth and personal transformation. Elul, as the final month of the spring/summer season is connected to endings. Elul gives us the strength to be able to finish strong, to end well. Elul also serves as a month of preparation for the New Year/Rosh Hashanah.

We inhale our past year, ending with wisdom and then we also gain the wisdom to begin anew and exhale a positive year into being. The mental, emotional, and spiritual objective of this month is introspection and the reclaiming of our inner purity and wholeness.

THE MONTH OF TISHREI:
A Time of Rebirth & Upward Movement

Each month of the year radiates with distinct Divine qualities and unique opportunities for growth and spiritual illumination. As Tishrei begins the new yearly cycle, it is an appropriate month to introspect, reflect and resolve to move forward and preserve moving forward into the more inward months of the winter. This month creates the space to unburden ourselves from our negativities, and enter a more sacred, grounded sacred space. In Tishrei we are given the gift of forgiveness and then the ability to truly regain our space and inner joy.

THE MONTH OF CHESHVAN:
Navigating Transitions, Elevating the Fall

Directly on the heels of the inspiring and holiday-filled month of Tishrei, Cheshvan is a month that is quiet and devoid of holidays. In the month of Cheshvan we use the stored up energies of the previous months to self-generate our inspiration and creativity and provide ourselves with the strength to rise up after a fall. In Cheshvan we are entering into a stormier, wetter and colder season. It is a month of transition. The mental, emotional and spiritual objective of this month is to weather the transitions, learn to self-generate and stand tall. And if we do fall, we use the quality of this month to get back up and do so with more conviction, strength, wisdom and clarity.

THE MONTH OF TEVES:

Refining Relationships, Elevating the Body

The quality of Teves is generally harsh—much like its counterpart Tamuz in the summer, thus the tendency for many is to hunker down, retract, curl up and wait for the month to pass by, only to reemerge when the harshness has dissipated.Think for a moment about the 'easier' months of the year, which, like gentle waves in the ocean, carry us where we want to go. We can ride these energies easily and they can propel us forward effortlessly, we just need to go with the overall flow, so to speak. The harsher months, on the other hand, can be compared to the more powerful waves that emanate from the belly of the ocean,which come forcefully crashing down and can easily drown a person before they even realize what has happened. However, those who want to utilize the momentum of the powerful energy that is available during such times can, with caution and creativity, harness these intense waves and ride them higher and farther than other, more gentle circumstances may allow. However, harnessing the power of Tohu, the raw energy of the body, does in fact need to be approached with great care and attention.

New Book!

THE MYSTERY OF SHABBOS

Shabbat Rediscovered

Delving into the transformative power of Shabbos. With an all-encompassing perspective that ranges from the literal, Pshat observation and Halachic implications of the texts, to the allegorical, the philosophical, and finally, to the deeper secrets as revealed by Kabbalah and Chassidus, creating an elegant tapestry of thought and experience. THE MYSTERY OF SHABBOS is a profound meditation on the meaning of Shabbos and demonstrates the physical, emotional, mental and spiritual possibilities available and given to us with the gift of Shabbos. Studying and contemplating this inspired text on the depths of Shabbos will unveil a redemptive light in your experience of the Seventh Day -- and by extension, every day of your life.

www.ingramcontent.com/pod-product-compliance
Lightning Source LLC
Chambersburg PA
CBHW060756100426
42813CB00004B/834

* 9 7 8 1 7 3 3 8 1 3 0 9 9 *